PAINT

Decorating with water-based paints

John Sutcliffe

Special photography by Andrew Twort

HENRY HOLT AND COMPANY
NEW YORK

This book is for Sebastian, Lucy, Tom and Laurence

Henry Holt and Company, Inc.
Publishers since 1866
115 West 18th Street
New York, New York 10011

Henry Holt® is a registered trademark of Henry Holt and Company, Inc.

Published in Canada by Fitzhenry & Whiteside Ltd.,
195 Allstate Parkway,
Markham, Ontario L3R 4T8.

Library of Congress Cataloging-in-Publication Data is available upon request.

ISBN 0-8050-4739-5

Henry Holt books are available for special promotions and premiums.
For details contact: Director, Special Markets.

First American Edition—1997

Printed in Italy

All first editions are printed on acid-free paper ∞

1 3 5 7 9 10 8 6 4 2

FRONTISPIECE *The uneven, chalky surface of distempered walls contrasts
with the smooth matte finish on the paneled doors, with their carefully delineated cream surrounds.*

Contents

The advantages of water-based paints 7

COLOR AND PIGMENT 10

Color theory and mixing 12   Adding color to paint 14   Red pigments 16
Yellow pigments 18   Blue pigments 20   Green pigments 22
Brown pigments 24   Black pigments 26   White pigments 27

PREPARATION 28

Preparing to paint 30   Order of painting 34   Equipment 38

DISTEMPER 40

Colorwashing 46   Sponging 50   Spattering 52
Trompe l'oeil stone blocks 54   Marbling 58
Two-stage sponge stamping 62   Freestyle painted garland 66

MILK PAINTS 70

Flat painting 76   Rubber stamping 78   Stenciling on walls 80
Stenciling on wood 86   Freestyle details 90

LATEX 94

Simple colorwashing 100   Colorwashing over sponging 104
Simple and layered sponging 108   Sponging stripes 110
Freestyle stripes and checks 112   Distressing wood 114
Pickled wood 116   Painted stenciling 118
Stenciling using a sponge 120   Trompe l'oeil tiles 124

ACRYLICS AND ARTISTS' PAINTS 128

Painting iron 134   Verdigris 136   Bronzed finish and gold leaf 138
Colorwashing and antiquing 140   Stippling and combing 142   Oak graining 144
Mahogany graining 146   Rosewood graining 148   Tortoiseshelling 150
Black and gold marbling 152   Pale marbling 154   Freestyle decoration 156

Suppliers 160   Suppliers' credits 164
Bibliography 164   Index 165   Acknowledgments 168

THE ADVANTAGES OF WATER-BASED PAINTS

I have always enjoyed using water-based paints. In the forty-five years that have elapsed since I watched my father turn our small bathroom into the interior of a fanciful tent (with gray-and-white striped wallpaper printed in distemper for the walls and ceiling, and coral-colored Walpamur oil-bound distemper for the scalloped lambrequins), the distinctive smell of that distemper has often returned to haunt me. It is a wholesome smell which, to me at any rate, conjures up immediately the silky smooth texture of the paint itself and my appreciation, even then, of the possibilities inherent in a pot of paint.

Water-based paints are pleasant to use. Some have been around for centuries and so have proved their worth, while modern water-based paints are the subject of constant research and improvement. They do not have the lingering smell that is the result of solvent evaporation – even though modern latex paint still contains approximately ten percent solvent. Water-based paints do not provoke headache or nausea. They are thinned with water. They dry fast, so they can be quickly recoated a second or third time if necessary. An added bonus is that equipment and hands can be cleaned with nothing more than soap and water, preventing skin from coming into contact with potentially harmful brush cleaners, and protecting water supplies from contamination.

These ecological considerations are important. In 1990 the World Watch Institute (an American research organization concerned with global problems) published a report stating that a fifth of the world's population breathes air contaminated beyond internationally agreed safety limits. This pollution is caused as much by everyday household substances as by the more obvious industrial processes that create, for example, acid rain. The production and use of one common household substance, namely paint, and especially oil paint, is proving to be a major pollutant. The various production processes involved in the manufacture of paint – such as extracting and refining the pigments and producing the oils and solvents – all create their own pollution problems, which

A traditional paint such as distemper is the ideal choice in a setting which relies for its charm on the texture of the walls. The darker paint on the risers and in bands at the side of the stairs, acting as a kind of baseboard, is better able to withstand the marks made when cleaning the staircase.

luckily in many countries are fairly well regulated by legislation. No longer are arsenic or mercury used in pigment-making. Lead paint is still produced, but under strictly controlled conditions, and in Britain regulations limit its use to historic buildings. Nowadays, it is the solvents or volatile organic compounds (VOCs) used in paint (and those used to clean up the mess after painting) that cause pollution problems. It is estimated that paint is responsible for eight percent of the VOCs emitted into the atmosphere.

All paint is made up of three main elements. The pigment provides the color and greater or lesser degrees of obliteration to cover up what is underneath. The binder sticks the pigment to the surface being painted. The vehicle, a liquid, dilutes the binder, making the whole mass brushable. This vehicle, which in the case of oil paint is a solvent, evaporates once the job is done. One shocking fact is that, on average, a pot of traditional oil paint containing 8¾ pt/5 lt will release 6½ lb/3-4 kg of solvent into the atmosphere as it dries. Paint solvent is similar to the solvents used in other everyday substances, such as glues, furniture polish, hairspray, nail varnish, lubricants, fabric softeners, and in the industrial cleaning and dry-cleaning industries. The action of sunlight on these released solvents combines with nitrogen oxide from vehicle exhausts to form ground-level ozone (summertime photochemical smog). Ozone can damage plants and materials and cause breathing difficulties for some people. At the same time, the solvents contribute to the depletion of the ozone layer and so in turn to the greenhouse effect, hence global warming. Solvent-based paint also affects humans directly at the time of use. Its fumes are breathed in or absorbed by the skin. Exposure to solvents can cause nausea, giddiness, headaches, breathlessness, and anxiety.

In addition to these pollution issues, there is the problem of waste paint disposal. In some countries, companies are required by law to treat their hazardous waste differently from general refuse. Householders, however, can in theory dispose of waste paint along with their normal household trash. Rather than being thrown away, surplus paint should be passed to someone else or mixed with other paint of a similar type and recolored if necessary. Such hazardous materials make up only about one percent of all household wastes, but the impact of even such small amounts can be felt. If paint and turpentine end up in landfill sites, their contents may leach into the soil and pollute groundwater.

The paint industry is going to great lengths to reduce the damage to the environment caused by its products. In the early 1980s, solvent made up fifty to seventy percent of oil paint. That figure has been reduced dramatically, but there is still room for improvement.

If paint and painting on both a domestic and an industrial scale are to be less damaging in the future than they have been over the last fifty years, the lessons of previous centuries must be learned and the simpler formulations of the past adopted or adapted. It may seem paradoxical, in the twentieth century, to be reverting to the use of water as the best vehicle for paint, for this is the oldest way of getting color onto a wall. The paint of the cave painters was created by collecting earth ground fine by a river, grinding it again, and making it brushable with water. The palette and methods of these early artists were simple, but the results were not so far removed from the various kinds of distemper that have been used ever since.

Oil paints in which the pigments are bound in oils and the vehicle is a solvent, such as turpentine, arrived on the scene later. They were certainly being used by decorators in the seventeenth century, but their supremacy was not firmly established until the nineteenth. Since then, it has been generally accepted that, while ceilings and walls are decorated in water paint, woodwork is painted in oil.

Now the wheel is turning full circle. In certain states, public buildings must by law be painted only with water-based paints. This is as it should be for the sake of our health and that of the planet. However, it is unlikely that oil paints will disappear completely – nor should they, for they are still the first choice for some situations. Just as modern lead paint is available for use in controlled circumstances, so manufacturers are now producing oil paints to new standards, using non-toxic oils and natural diluents.

For too long now, water-based paints have been regarded as a poor relation, incapable of producing anything other than the simplest plain painting. In this book I show that all kinds of effects, simple and complex, are possible with water-based paints. These effects are sometimes, but not always, similar to those of traditional oil paint. They provide an alternative vocabulary for the decorator who wishes to use water-based products for their speed, cleanliness, and for their well-documented environmental advantages.

Water-based paints can be used to produce effects of great subtlety. Here, latex in various shades of blue-green has been colorwashed onto walls to create glowing depth of color. The crisp white woodwork and ceiling provide a good foil for this painterly treatment.

Color

and

pigment

COLOR THEORY AND MIXING

There are three primary colors as shown on the most basic color wheel – red, blue, and yellow – and three secondaries – green, orange, and violet. It is theoretically possible to mix any color from the primaries: green from yellow and blue; orange from red and yellow; and violet from red and blue. The snag, as anyone who has tried will have discovered, is that this does not always work, and mixing from these three primaries often results in a gray-brown mess. The first question is, if you are trying to mix all colors from red, blue, and yellow, which red, blue, and yellow should you choose? There are cool blue-reds and warm orange-reds, cool green-blues, warm blues that lean toward violet, and cool green-yellows as well as warm orange-yellows. No pigment produces absolutely pure, neutral primaries. Instead, every color has the potential to be either a cool or a warm version of the hue, and each version should be treated as a separate color. For mixing the best possible range of colors, two sorts of each primary color are needed – one warm and one cool. When a cool acid yellow, such as lemon yellow, is mixed with a cool blue, such as Prussian blue, the result will be a pure cold green, but an orange-yellow, such as cadmium yellow, mixed with a warm blue like ultramarine, will result in a warm green that has some brown in its make-up.

In some color wheels which show a range of intermediate colors, the fact that the color wheel has a cool side and a warm side becomes more obvious. The cool yellows, greens, blues, and cool violets all lie next to each other on one side of the wheel. If they are combined together in a decorating scheme, the result will be a harmonious one. Opposite and, again, next to each other are the warm yellows, oranges, reds, and warm violets. When they are combined they will also provide harmony. Even this further division of the wheel into a cool and warm side is an oversimplification, for on the cool side of the wheel there are colors that are comparatively warm and vice versa. A cool yellow may still have some orange in it, or the "potential" for orange, which means that, if mixed with blue, it can give a warm olive green rather than a cool lime green. Conversely, a warm yellow may have some "potential" for blue, which means that, if mixed with blue, it can create a cool green.

The colors opposite each other on the color wheel – red opposite green, yellow opposite violet, and orange opposite blue – are known as complementaries. The impact of any color is increased by the presence of even a small quantity of its complementary; if blue, for instance, is placed next to orange, the blue will seem bluer and the orange more orange. This effect can be used to enhance the impact of a color in a room – a blue-painted chair and blue curtains placed in a predominantly orange room, for example, will create a contrasting scheme rather than a harmonious one. Brown has the "potential" for red or green, because it is a mixture of these two complementaries. The rule about complementaries enhancing one another applies here, too: if brown is placed beside green, the red of the brown will be emphasized, but, put next to red, the green will be enhanced, and the red suppressed. In mixing colors, something different happens. We see that a paint is yellow, for example, because it absorbs most of the light waves that are not yellow, and reflects back the yellow ones. Mixing some violet into yellow will make the yellow less intense, since the resulting color will also reflect some violet light waves. It is as if the color is trying to destroy its complementary. Mixing complementaries together in roughly equal proportions will result in a brownish color, as one will cancel the other out. Similarly, a red wall brushed over with a glaze or wash of green will assume a brownish hue and more coats of glaze will make it browner.

TONES AND TINTS

Colors are not limited only to those seen on a simple color wheel. On the contrary, for every color, or hue, there are also tones and tints of that color. Tone is the relative lightness or darkness of a color as seen against a scale of black through gray to white. A tint of a color is created by adding white. For instance, if more white is added progressively to a blue, the result will be a range of blue tints from the vivid to a pale, less brilliant blue. If colors have very dissimilar tonal qualities, there will be a sharp contrast between them. At its most extreme, black contrasts strongly with white. Some reds and greens, however, are similar tonally, so that when they are seen next to each other, we are not struck by any strong tonal contrast.

Tone is an important consideration when choosing colors for decoration. For example, if a strong tonal contrast between woodwork and walls is wanted, dark brown woodwork against pale gray or blue walls is a possibility. Alternatively, white woodwork against pale green walls would give less tonal contrast and might be preferred for its soothing effect. Colors can also be made to seem darker or lighter according to how they are placed. Beige woodwork will look dark against off-white walls, but if the walls are recoated pure white, the same woodwork will appear to be much darker. By the same token, dark cream walls will look lighter when the woodwork is painted a dark, strong blue than when it is painted white.

LIGHTENING AND DARKENING COLORS

The obvious way to lighten, or produce a lighter tint of a color, is to add white, as with the blue/white mixture described above. However, if you use a thin wash of blue over a white background, the blue will remain as intensely blue as the original, although it will be paler in tone. A third alternative is to use the blue as a base with a thin wash of white on top. The white wash will cloud the blue and create a color that is less intense than the original even when it is of the same tonality as the blue wash over a white background.

The simplest way to darken the color of a paint is to add more of the same color. An alternative is to add black, but care should be taken as this reduces color saturation. The third, subtle, option is to paint the color over a darker background. This alternative offers a variety of effects. Blue washed or ragrolled over a darker gray, for instance, will look quite different from the same blue applied over black. The effects produced by the different options are illustrated by the samples on the right.

White in medium used as a glaze over the basic mix

Basic mix in medium used as a glaze over white

Basic mix + white

Basic mix: phthalo blue + raw umber + white

Basic mix + black + phthalo blue

Basic mix in medium used as a glaze over black

ADDING COLOR TO PAINT

For many, ready-mixed paints provide the most convenient material for decoration. However, since growing numbers of people enjoy mixing their own paint, it is useful to know something about the composition of paint. Paint consists of three elements: the medium or vehicle, the binder, and the pigment. The medium makes the mixture brushable. The binder, which hardens as water evaporates, anchors the paint to the surface. The pigments provide color and covering power. All the paints discussed in this book have water as their medium or vehicle. In the case of distemper, the binder is size, with additional linseed oil in oil-bound distemper; in milk paints it is casein; in latex and acrylic paint it is acrylic. Pigment can be added either in the form of solid matter or as stainers.

The story of pigments is long and complicated, and the subject of considerable research. It is difficult to know which pigments were used in the past by artists and which were used by decorators. Many traditional pigments were poisonous, either in manufacture, or use, or both. Lead pigments and the green in a wallpaper that is supposed to have killed Napoleon are two examples. As children we were taught not to lick our brushes when painting, but today there are strict rules about the use of toxic pigments.

Pigments for coloring paint used in decoration are available as pure pigments, stainers, powder color, gouache and poster paints, and acrylics.

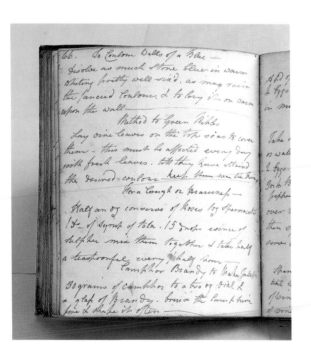

In this old English recipe book dating from the eighteenth century, a housewife has recorded a method for making distemper alongside various household remedies.

PURE PIGMENTS

Sold in powder form by weight, pure pigments do not contain any binder. They come in an enormous choice of colors. Some, such as vermilion and pure ultramarine, are expensive because of the cost of their raw ingredients (see pp16 and 20), and they are not often used in house decoration. The ochers and other earth colors are much cheaper and have been used for centuries in decoration the world over. When adding pigment to a liquid, you should first mix it with water in a small container and then add it, in solution, to the rest of the medium. Be careful to avoid bubbles of paint forming around knots of powder. As lamp black (see p26) will not dissolve completely in water due to its greasy nature, it should first be mixed with denatured alcohol and then added to the rest of the paint, where the alcohol will happily combine with the water.

STAINERS

Stainers are color without a binder and are sold as a thickish liquid in tubes and plastic bottles. The colors are all synthetic and very powerful. The selection of colors is limited, but is usually enough for most people's requirements. Stainers are easy to use as they do not need to be prediluted. Water stainers suitable for use only in water-based paint are best, but they can only be bought from specialist stores or ordered from suppliers. Universal stainers are suitable for use in either oil- or water-based paint and are more widely available, but they are a second choice to water stainers. When coloring distemper, you should certainly buy a water stainer; it is lime-friendly, so the color is not affected by the lime in the mix.

The only possible disadvantage of stainers is that, having no binder and hence no drying power of their own, they slow down the drying time of the paint. Used excessively, they could make an unstable paint incapable of drying. The amount that can be safely incorporated will vary according to the kind of stainer, so you should always check the manufacturer's instructions before use. These commercially available stainers are the same as those used to mix paints in paint stores, where they are added to cans of paint with sufficient binders. The dark colors are mixed in a special base which contains less white content than the paler base. This deep base paint can be purchased uncolored, and you can add color in the form of stainers to make a useful paint glaze for top-coating walls in medium or pale tones.

POWDER COLORS

These are the familiar school paints, used in the classroom. They consist of pigment mixed with a water-soluble binder. As the pigment is not usually of very good quality, the colors are not always stable, but they are inexpensive and sold in most artists' suppliers. They come in a limited but useful choice of colors and must be mixed with water before being added to the paint.

GOUACHE AND POSTER PAINTS

These are colors mixed with a binder, usually size, more rarely casein. They are obtained from artists' suppliers. As those bound with size are a form of distemper, they can be re-wetted. However, this means that they will "wake up" under the brush, making them hard to paint over. The casein-bound variety is virtually waterproof, allowing overpainting. Both types, being rich in pigment, are a valuable if expensive source of color. Sold as a paste in pots or tubes, gouache and poster paints come in a huge selection of strong colors. Their purity makes them ideal for coloring glazes. As they are comparatively expensive, they are unsuitable for large quantities of strong color, but being finely ground and smooth, they are ideal for stenciling and graining. Gouache and poster paints have plenty of body and remain substantial even when diluted. They should be diluted before they are added to the paint.

ACRYLICS

Acrylics, which are pigments in an acrylic binder, are sold in tubes in a wide choice of colors, and are also usually bought from specialist art suppliers. As with gouache, the price varies according to the color. The acrylic binder allows them to dry very hard, making them resistant to wear and damp. Acrylics are also good for freestyle painting, for they can be glazed or overpainted without "waking up". Acrylics are particularly suitable for coloring latex paints and acrylic glazes. They may be added to distemper, but bear in mind that they strengthen the distemper, making it unsuitable for using as a top coat over a base coat of soft distemper as the previous coat will tend to mix with it. You should dilute acrylics before adding them to paint or glaze.

COVERING POWER

The covering power or opacity of a paint is determined by the translucency of the pigments used and by the proportion of pigment in the mixture. Many paints nowadays are largely made up of the pigment titanium white (see p27), which, along with black, is very opaque. Many of the earth colors like yellow ocher (see p18) and burnt sienna (see p25) are fairly transparent. In much house decoration, opacity is useful for covering up old coats of paint with as little effort as possible. For subtler effects, it is best if the last coat or coats are translucent enough to allow the color of the lower coat to show through. To make paint translucent, it can be thinned, either with water or with a mixture of water and medium, such as acrylic medium. Water alone might result in a mix that does not adhere well and runs. Instead, to make an exceptionally translucent top coat, mix a large quantity of water and acrylic medium with a very small amount of color.

The rate of dilution required will depend on many factors, including the texture and absorbency of the wall and of the various undercoats. Two people can paint a wall using the same brush and the same pot of paint and yet produce different effects. For this reason, it is not possible to give precise recipes for mixing the paints used in the various projects described in this book. A general rule to remember is that it should never be hard work to apply paint. Two thin coats will go on much more easily and with better results than one over-thick coat.

TESTING COLORS

The best place to test color mixes or the effect of colorwashes is on the surface for which they are planned. You will be able to judge the effect in different lights and against furnishings or fabric swatches. Once you have decided on a color, you should paint these patches out before starting work. An alternative, especially suitable for trying out layered glazes, is to use large boards. Prime and treat them with exactly the same paint as you plan to use on the finished surface. You will need to test your colors as you mix them, too, but the exact effect can only be judged once the color is dry. Initially, mix only a small quantity – a teaspoonful is usually enough. Paint these samples onto white postcards. Dry them with a hairdryer, set to give plenty of cool air, and avoid too much heat, which can distort the color. Once you have decided on the colors, these postcards make useful color swatches to carry with you if you have to match fabrics or carpets. Color mixes are given for each of the projects described in this book, but the exact proportions are not specified. This is because it is largely a matter of trial and error, and individual preference. The more you experiment with such mixing, the easier it is to attain the desired shade.

RED PIGMENTS

Pigments giving red hues have been used for centuries by artists and house decorators the world over – in ancient Egyptian tomb paintings, medieval manuscripts, Chinese temples, and the barns of colonial America. As with other pigments, reds can be obtained from a variety of sources, animal, vegetable, mineral, and of course the earth itself, which yields a wide range of red ocher pigments. Depending on the place of origin, red earth colors – deriving from iron deposits in the soil – range from orange-reds through to purple-reds. As with all the earth colors, their ready availability traditionally made them especially suitable for house decoration, when they would be combined in a wash with chalk or lime. Indian red and Venetian red are two of the most useful red earth pigments. Venetian red may originally have come from Venice or have reached Europe via Venice, while Indian red, which was more highly prized, came originally from the island of Ormus in the Persian Gulf, but

Red earth is exactly what its name suggests – earth with a reddish hue. Here it is shown in its raw form and powdered, ready to be mixed with a suitable medium such as water, milk, or oil.

When mixing red-based colors, you should always consider how much blue the red contains. No amount of yellow will turn a crimson orange. Similarly, blue will turn an orange-red brown, not purple.

Venetian red

Indian red
A purplish-red, Indian red was originally the name given to an imported earth red, but by the eighteenth century, it was being widely manufactured. It is a useful decorators' color of great durability.

Indian red

Venetian red
Originally made from a native earth, by the eighteenth century Venetian red was being produced as a manufactured iron oxide. Early in the nineteenth century, it was recorded as being used to paint imitation mahogany.

Venetian red + white

Venetian red + Indian red

Indian red + white

Venetian red + yellow ocher

Venetian red + yellow ocher + white

Venetian red + Indian red + white

was a name also used by early American painters to describe the earth color used by Native Americans.

The animal and vegetable sources of red pigments include the female *Coccus lacca,* an insect that infests trees in Asia and India. It can be crushed to produce Indian lake, while the cochineal insect from South America – *Coccus cacti* – produces what was the most expensive pigment of the eighteenth and nineteenth centuries – carmine, along with a red lake, sometimes called Venetian lake. In general, the lakes are expensive and tend to fade, but they give bright, transparent colors; and early in the nineteenth century, they were recommended as one of the best sources of color for glazing and for wood graining and marbling. They remained popular with decorators until the late nineteenth century.

Vegetable sources for reds include brasil or pernambuco wood, and redwood, while another vegetable source used since early times is the madder plant. This makes a bluish-red that is not very permanent. Early in the nineteenth century, extraction of the dye

alizarin from the madder plant was perfected, and that is when "madder" came into common use as a pigment name.

Mineral sources for reds include cinnabar, used in antiquity to produce a bright red; lead, to make red lead, which is cheap but lacks permanence; and cadmium, the silvery metal discovered in 1817.

But, as with pigments other than red, many of the naturally occurring ingredients needed are prohibitively expensive, difficult to extract, or rare. Centuries ago, people found that many could be made more cheaply by chemical manufacture, and this practice has continued to the present day. Vermilion has been produced from sulfur and mercury since the early medieval period. Nowadays, cadmium red is the usual substitute. In the eighteenth century, Indian red was hard to come by, so it was made from iron oxide. Once a method for manufacturing synthetic alizarin was perfected in 1868, it quickly replaced the natural alizarin of the madder plant, giving a pigment that can produce many reds, ranging from scarlet to maroon.

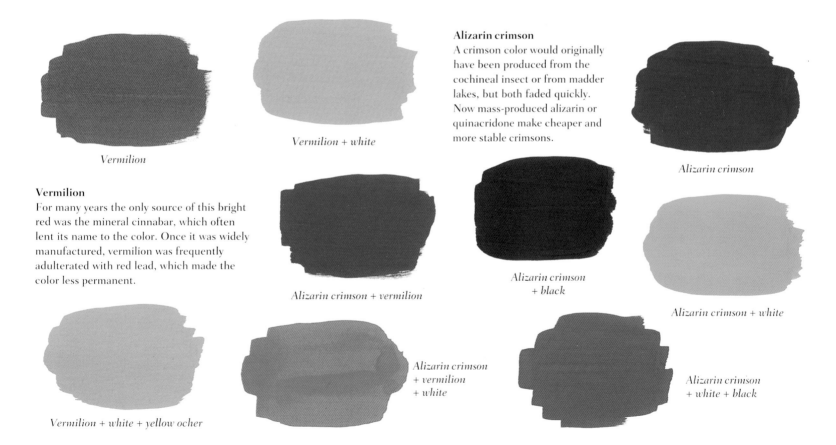

Vermilion

Vermilion + white

Alizarin crimson
A crimson color would originally have been produced from the cochineal insect or from madder lakes, but both faded quickly. Now mass-produced alizarin or quinacridone make cheaper and more stable crimsons.

Alizarin crimson

Vermilion
For many years the only source of this bright red was the mineral cinnabar, which often lent its name to the color. Once it was widely manufactured, vermilion was frequently adulterated with red lead, which made the color less permanent.

Alizarin crimson + vermilion

Alizarin crimson + black

Alizarin crimson + white

Vermilion + white + yellow ocher

Alizarin crimson + vermilion + white

Alizarin crimson + white + black

YELLOW PIGMENTS

A resin laboriously gathered from trees, gamboge derives its name from Cambodia, its place of origin. Like most vegetable yellows, it is very fugitive.

Yellow ochers, which are clay colored by iron oxide, give the cheap and permanent soft gold yellows which have always been used for house decoration. They are found in many parts of the world. England, France, Holland, and Siena in Italy all produce yellow ocher. Mars yellow is an artificial yellow ocher. It is very permanent and gives more brilliant hues than the natural earth yellows.

Some yellow pigments can be derived from organic sources, but many are fugitive, which means that they fade easily. Saffron is a deep yellow produced from the stamens of *Crocus sativus*. Gamboge, derived from the gum resin of an evergreen tree in Southeast Asia, was in use from medieval times to the nineteenth century. Indian yellow was made from the concentrated urine of cows force-fed on mango leaves. People's sensibilities about the malnourished condition of the animals were outraged when the true origin of the pigment became known, and production stopped in the 1920s.

Any yellow that resembled gold has traditionally been of interest

Yellow is a light color which is best used as a glaze, where its subtleties can be best appreciated. Good cool yellows can be mixed from lemon yellow or cadmium yellow light, and warm yellows from yellow ocher and cadmium yellow deep.

Yellow ocher

Lemon yellow

Lemon yellow
Lemon yellow is a useful, cool green-yellow with no hint of the orange contained by some other yellows. This makes it especially good for mixing pure greens and sharp pale yellows.

Yellow ocher + white

Yellow ocher
Before the days when good green paints were available, yellow ocher, mixed with Prussian blue, provided the best and cheapest green for house decoration. Artists value it, too, for its brushability, ease of mixing, and soft golden yellow color.

Lemon yellow + white

Lemon yellow + black

Yellow ocher + black

Yellow ocher + lemon yellow

Yellow ocher + lemon yellow + white

to artists and decorators. The mineral orpiment – yellow sulfide of arsenic – was one such pigment, known since early times. It was found in Holland, Germany, and Italy, and later, in the nineteenth century, large quantities were imported from China under the name Chinese yellow. Unfortunately, the pigment had an unpleasant smell and gave off dangerous fumes. By contrast with the warm yellow of orpiment, lemon yellow, available since the first half of the nineteenth century, offers a sharp, acidic cool lemon color. The term today often simply signifies a pale cool yellow hue rather than a particular ingredient, and the lemon yellows of different manufacturers all differ slightly.

A number of other traditional yellows were based on lead. Naples yellow or lead antimolliate has been made since the fifteenth century. For a long time, people believed it came from the slopes of Vesuvius, hence its name. Naples yellow became very popular in the late eighteenth century, and was often used with blue to make a good green. Patent yellow was lead oxychloride, a bright yellow pigment now obsolete. Patented in 1781 by James Turner, it was often called Turner's yellow. Since yellow was fashionable for house decoration in Europe in the late Adam to early Empire periods, patent yellow was sometimes used, but it was damaged by polluted town air and sunlight. Decorators used it in an oil medium, and it was popular with coach painters, who applied it in a varnish medium or as base coat for chrome yellow.

Chrome yellow was another lead-based yellow, discovered at the end of the eighteenth century. By the 1820s, there was a good enough supply of lead chromate for chrome yellow to be made on a large scale. It caught on almost immediately, especially with house painters, because a little went a long way. Unlike orpiment, chrome yellow was not poisonous, and it had the advantage of making a beautiful green when mixed with Prussian blue.

The metal cadmium was discovered in 1817, but because it was in short supply, cadmium yellow was not immediately available commercially. The cadmium yellows range from a pale, cool lemon color to a deep version which is almost bright orange. They all have good covering power.

Cadmium yellows
All the cadmium yellows are prized for their opacity. They are available as cadmium yellow light, cadmium yellow medium, and cadmium yellow deep. While the light versions may have a bias toward green, the deep ones are orange-yellows.

Cadmium yellow light

Cadmium yellow deep

Cadmium yellow deep + white

Cadmium yellow light + white

Cadmium yellow deep + cadmium yellow light

Cadmium yellow deep + yellow ocher

Cadmium yellow light + white + black

Cadmium yellow deep + cadmium yellow light + white

Cadmium yellow deep + lemon yellow + white

Cadmium yellow deep + yellow ocher + white

Ground and cleansed of its impurities, lapis lazuli retains the magic of the original stone. It has been equaled as a pigment in modern times by manufactured French ultramarine.

There are cool and warm blues. When cool blues such as Prussian blue are set against warm ones like ultramarine, they can almost seem different hues. The green-blue turquoises are so far from the nearly purple blues that, when used together, they can "buzz" in the same way that red and green do when used next to each other.

BLUE PIGMENTS

One of the first artificial pigments was blue. Frit – a blue ceramic glaze made from copper silicates – was used in Egypt from about 3000 B.C. Knowledge of the processes employed in producing this glaze spread to ancient Crete and Rome.

Ultramarine, the most expensive artists' pigment, made from the semiprecious stone lapis lazuli, was first introduced to Europe in the twelfth century. It was produced by crushing the stone under water with a paste of wax, resin, and oil. The blue particles floated into the water while the other minerals remained in the paste. Lapis lazuli is found in mountainous, inaccessible parts of the world, including Afghanistan, China, Chile, and Persia. Demand for this color has always exceeded supply, hence the high price – at times it cost as much as gold. In the early nineteenth century, a mysterious blue color was observed in the furnaces producing soda ash. After many experiments, the French manufacturer Guimet found that an artificial ultramarine could be produced by heating clay, soda, sulfur, and coal. Since 1828, this process has been used in the

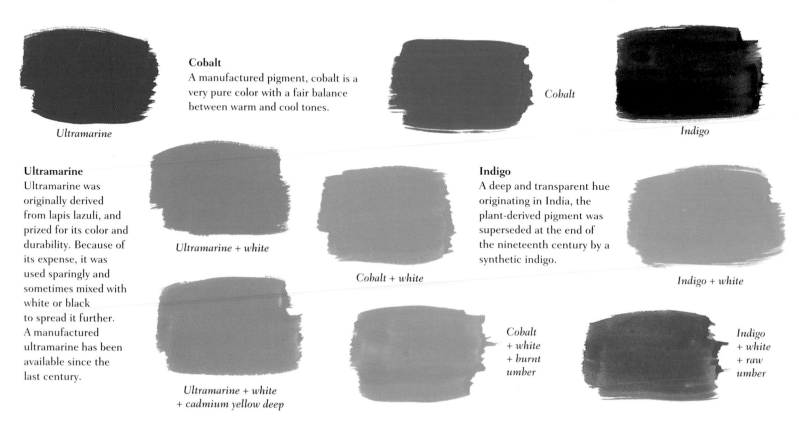

Cobalt
A manufactured pigment, cobalt is a very pure color with a fair balance between warm and cool tones.

Ultramarine

Cobalt

Indigo

Ultramarine
Ultramarine was originally derived from lapis lazuli, and prized for its color and durability. Because of its expense, it was used sparingly and sometimes mixed with white or black to spread it further. A manufactured ultramarine has been available since the last century.

Ultramarine + white

Cobalt + white

Indigo
A deep and transparent hue originating in India, the plant-derived pigment was superseded at the end of the nineteenth century by a synthetic indigo.

Indigo + white

Ultramarine + white + cadmium yellow deep

Cobalt + white + burnt umber

Indigo + white + raw umber

commercial production of French ultramarine. The two pigments, the natural lapis and the artificial ultramarine, can only be distinguished under a microscope.

Manufactured in Saxony, the Netherlands, and France, smalt was another popular blue pigment. This rich warm blue was produced by crushing cobalt silicates, but the color became paler the more finely it was ground. By the eighteenth century, cobalt was quite expensive, but was still used by decorators especially on ironwork, usually as a scattering of blue color over the still-tacky white-lead paint. Before 1828, and the advent of artificial ultramarine, artists needing a cheaper blue often turned to azurite, a natural copper carbonate found in Hungary, Germany, and Central America. The color was important in European art from the fifteenth to seventeenth centuries, despite the fact that it sometimes had a green cast, and tended to become very pale when finely ground. Azurite was hardly ever used in house painting. Manufactured azurite, a byproduct of the refining of silver, was called blue verditer. For some reason, instead of a blue pigment, green was often the result of the production process. Cheap to produce in bulk, blue verditer was used by house decorators, particularly in distemper. In the early years of the nineteenth century, a London colorman recommended blue verditer for painting ceilings.

The chance discovery of Prussian blue, around 1710, marked the start of modern pigment manufacture. Diesbach, a Berlin color-maker, was making crimson lake when he happened to use some potash contaminated by animal waste and produced a deep blue. Its main drawback is a slight green tinge, but house painters of the early nineteenth century counteracted this by mixing it with a very small quantity of white, which had the additional advantage of increasing the Prussian blue's covering power. Phthalocyanine blue was first manufactured in 1935. Its color and covering power are similar to those of Prussian blue, with few of the disadvantages.

Thanks to the popularity of denim, indigo is famous as a blue pigment worldwide. Derived from *Indigofera*, a plant cultivated in India, it gives a good, deep, transparent blue, but is not very permanent. Modern synthetic indigo, which is sulfur-based, is not permanent either, as lovers of washed-out jeans will know.

Prussian blue
After its discovery in the eighteenth century, Prussian blue became popular with artists and house painters. A tenth the price of ultramarine, it was not poisonous, mixed easily, and was reasonably permanent.

Prussian blue

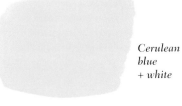

Cerulean blue

Phthalocyanine blue
Phthalocyanine blue is the modern replacement for Prussian blue. Discovered in Scotland in 1935 and marketed a year later, it was first observed as an impurity when a dye vat cracked. The color has very strong staining powers and, like its relative phthalocyanine green, can easily dominate a room.

Cerulean blue
This cool, opaque sky blue has excellent covering power. It is expensive, so its use tends to be restricted to the decoration of small objects. Its strength makes it useful for painting furniture.

Prussian blue + white

Cerulean blue + white

Phthalo blue

Prussian blue + white + raw umber

Cerulean blue + white + raw umber

Phthalo blue + white

GREEN PIGMENTS

One green pigment dug from the ground is green earth, or *terre verte*, produced from a green clay containing iron and manganese. The best source of this green was Bohemia, whose clay gives a pure green, but suitable clays were also found in Italy, France, and Cyprus.

In use from Roman times until the nineteenth century, verdigris was one of the earliest manufactured pigments, commercially produced in France in the seventeenth century from red wine, grape stalks, and copper. As verdigris was cheap to produce, it was popular with dyers and house decorators, the latter using it in oil or distemper. Green verditer – often produced in error instead of blue verditer (see p21) – is a manufactured version of the mineral malachite, or green copper carbonate. The name verditer comes from the Old French *verd de terre,* meaning "green of the earth."

Malachite is a beautiful semi-precious stone, whose green color derives from copper. It was used to make a bright green pigment until the end of the eighteenth century.

The most striking greens always possess a translucent quality which can be accentuated by using them as glazes. More solid greens, such as olive green mixed from Prussian blue and yellow ocher, give a feeling of sobriety. The brightest greens contain a high proportion of yellow.

Emerald green

Emerald green + white

Phthalo green

Terre verte

Emerald green
The original emerald pigment in use in the early nineteenth century was highly toxic, but the modern synthetic version is perfectly safe to use. Emerald is a bright cool and yellowish green with excellent covering power.

Emerald green + white + vermilion

Phthalocyanine green
Phthalocyanine green – closely related to phthalocyanine blue – is a very permanent synthetic green whose chemical name is chlorinated copper phthalocyanine.

Terre verte
Terre verte was always popular in Italy for tempera and fresco painting. It was also adopted in house decoration: an early nineteenth-century decorators' manual described its use in distemper, but recommends that when used in oil it should be mixed with a large proportion of white lead.

Terre verte + white

Phthalo green + white

Phthalo green + white + cadmium yellow deep

Although coarse and lacking in covering power, it produced a light sea-green, regarded in the early nineteenth century as a good color for attics and meeting rooms – inevitably in distemper.

Green pigments produced from plants are, perhaps surprisingly, few and far between. Sap green, a dull green originally made from buckthorn berries, is the only such pigment whose name survives, though nowadays it refers to a synthetic pigment. Despite its tendency to turn brown and fade, it was a popular artists' pigment in the eighteenth century. Sap green is harmless, but some green pigments are not. Scheele's green was first made in 1775. Very poisonous, it was much used in ships' cabins. One wonders how many able seamen were disabled by it. The pigment with the worst reputation is emerald or Schweinfurt green, once used to remove barnacles from the hulls of boats and, under the name Paris green, sold as an insecticide. It is made from verdigris and arsenic, hence its poisonous nature. Its beautiful color must be the only reason for its survival. From 1814, when it was first produced commercially in Austria, it quickly became fashionable for house decoration. The dust from wallpaper printed with emerald green was once thought to have killed Napoleon. A slightly later development was viridian, a green oxide of chromium first made in Paris in 1838. As inferior grades of this pigment sometimes contain impurities, artists are usually recommended other, better-quality pigments.

Modern manufactured pigments do not suffer from the same drawbacks as some of the older ones. Phthalocyanine green is one example. A strong blue-green, it is very light-fast and popular as an artists' pigment today. Some people find it too garish and prefer to use the older, subtler green pigments. Intense dark greens are not easy to find in ready-mixed form. They are best made by blending together blue, yellow, and black and excluding white.

Although green pigments are widely available, many people prefer to mix their greens from yellows and blues. It is worth remembering that blues and yellows with a tendency to red will produce brownish greens, while sharper greens can be mixed from the cooler blues and yellows.

Prussian blue + lemon yellow

Indigo + lemon yellow

Indigo + cadmium yellow light

Prussian blue + lemon yellow + white

Prussian blue + cadmium yellow deep

Cerulean blue + cadmium yellow light + white

Prussian blue + yellow ocher

Prussian blue + yellow ocher + white

Prussian blue + cadmium yellow light

Phthalocyanine blue + lemon yellow

23

BROWN PIGMENTS

Earth colors have long been a staple part of the painters' and decorators' palette. Burnt umber was adopted as an artists' pigment as early as the first quarter of the seventeenth century and is still a popular and useful pigment today.

Naturally occurring clays and earths give a wide range of subtle browns. The color varies, according to the proportions of iron oxide and manganese present, between yellow, brown, and red. These many browns have been used since earliest times: they are the principal pigments in cave paintings. Easily procured and produced, these permanent colors are used throughout the world.

The range of ochers is very wide, varying from yellowish to reddish, with some even appearing grayish or greenish. Yellow ocher is the palest, while brown ocher is darker. Records exist of ochers having been produced in large quantities from the seventeenth century on, but because they were rather coarse, they were not popular with artists. To decorators, however, they were invaluable.

Umber is another brown earth color. In its raw state it has a slight cast of yellow, green, or even violet. The usual and most useful raw umber is that with a greenish-gray cast. The best quality comes from

A range of browns from cool to warm can be mixed from the basic earth pigments. Brown is also easily created – sometimes accidentally – by mixing together other colors. Those that lie opposite or nearly opposite each other on the color wheel will, when mixed, produce browns.

Burnt umber
This is the richest dark brown available. Mixed with white, it produces a pinky beige; with black it can produce subtle dark grays.

Raw umber

Burnt umber

Raw umber + white

Raw umber + white + yellow ocher

Burnt umber + black

Burnt umber + white

Raw umber
The name umber comes from the Latin *umbra*, meaning shadow. Decorators have traditionally used it in oil and distemper to achieve a stone color.

Raw umber + white + cadmium yellow light

Burnt umber + white + yellow ocher

Burnt umber + white + black

Cyprus. Burnt umber is raw umber that has been burnt. As with other "burnt" colors, it is warmer than the raw pigment. The semi-transparent nature of raw umber makes it ideal for creating glazes and for graining.

Sienna is an especially transparent clay found near Siena in Italy. It does not appear to have been given this name until the middle of the eighteenth century. Certainly by the early nineteenth century sienna was popular with house decorators, who liked it both in distemper and glaze. Like umber, it can be used either in its raw or burnt state, when it takes on a rich red mahogany color. Burnt and raw sienna mixed together produce a range of rich orange colors.

Nowadays the Mars colors – artificial iron oxides – can replace natural brown earths. They are very reliable as far as strength of color and light-fastness are concerned, but lack the subtlety of their natural counterparts. In their search for browns, pigment manufacturers have ranged widely among the possibilities of nature. Vandyke brown – apparently so named because the painter Van

Dyck liked the pigment so much – is a dark, rather transparent brown made from deposits of peat. The variety of pigment used by Van Dyck may have been better than modern Vandyke brown, which is now regarded as a fast-fading color, especially when used as a thin wash.

Sea life provides another source of brown pigment. The contents of just one ink sac from a cuttlefish will turn a thousand gallons of water opaque in seconds. The strong tinting quality of the sepia pigment has long been appreciated by artists. Nowadays, the sepia sold is usually a mixture of brown and black.

Perhaps the most macabre source of any color were Egyptian mummies, which yielded a brown pigment, originally taken for medicinal purposes. Bits of mummy were ground to make a pigment which, despite its fugitive nature, was popular with painters. It was sold under the name Egyptian brown. Surprisingly, it was not until the nineteenth century that the source of the pigment became generally known. This quickly led to its disappearance.

Sepia
Called sepia from the Italian *seppia,* meaning cuttlefish, the deep brown pigment that can be obtained from the ink sacs is particularly good for shading in *trompe l'oeil* work.

Sepia

Burnt sienna

Burnt sienna + white

Sepia + white

Raw sienna
Raw sienna gives a deep rich yellow with a strange latent "pinkiness" which is often, disconcertingly, revealed by the addition of white. Raw sienna can be used in graining to mimic satinwood or maple. In marbling it is used to produce Siena marble.

Burnt sienna + black

Burnt sienna
Burnt sienna is so fiery that it is sometimes classed as a red. Because of its rich mahogany color, house decorators of the early nineteenth century used it to mimic that wood.

Sepia + white + yellow ocher

Raw sienna

Raw sienna + white

Burnt sienna + white + yellow ocher

BLACK PIGMENTS

Black chalk from Würzburg in Germany was once ground to provide pigment, but is now more generally used as a drawing material. Most black pigments are produced by burning materials and so are carbon-based.

Like whites, blacks can depart a long way from an essential "blackness" before they are called by a different name. In decorating, blacks are more commonly used as elements in color mixes than on their own, although pure black is indispensable in black and gold marbling.

Soot, deposited by a smoking fire, was, with the earth pigments, probably one of the first colors used by our ancestors in their cave paintings. Lamp black is a pigment made from the soot produced by burning oils or fats. It came to be one of the standard black pigments, much appreciated for its permanency. As the soot is naturally fine and light, it does not need grinding for use as a pigment; but being rather greasy – a property shared with all carbon blacks – it dries slowly. Lamp black is more commonly mixed in oil paint than in watercolor because in water the pigment has a tendency to float. To avoid a similar problem when using lamp black in distemper, decorators should mix the dry pigment with denatured alcohol before adding it to the paint.

The mesolithic cooking fire yielded not only soot but charcoal and burnt bones, which could also be used to make black pigments. Ivory black, made from charred offcuts of ivory from the manufacture of items such as combs, was a very fine pigment of a deep, rich hue. Its name is a relic of the time before the modern ban on the trade in ivory. Bone black, essentially the same as ivory black, was much used in the eighteenth and nineteenth centuries, usually as a coarser and cheaper substitute for ivory black. Ivory black was, possibly because of the value of the raw material, always produced to a high standard and so was highly thought of for fine work. In the late eighteenth and early nineteenth centuries, decorators found the transparent qualities of ivory black useful in wood graining.

Burnt fruit stones were sometimes used for pigments, peach stones producing one of a particularly fine quality. Vine black, from charred vine stems, gave a bluish-black which was much prized by medieval artists. However, it could not be used in frescoes, as its tendency to draw out soluble salts from the plaster left unsightly efflorescence. Charred willow and other twigs produce charcoal, which, in powdered form, makes a poor paint pigment. A pigment known as printer's black was made from burnt wine lees mixed with some ivory or fruit-stone black. A similar color was achieved by Chinese or India inks, sometimes preferred to printer's black.

Modern black pigments include aniline black, carbon black, and Mars black. Aniline black was the first of the dyes to be derived from coal tar. Although it produces a good black, it fades badly and is of limited use. Mars black, an artificial oxide of iron, produces a color ranging from blue-gray to black which is opaque, light-fast, and very satisfactory.

Black + ultramarine

Black + vermilion

Black + white + crimson

Black + white

Black + white + yellow ocher

Black + white + burnt sienna

WHITE PIGMENTS

The search for a reliable white pigment obsessed the trade until the early years of this century. Anything white that came to hand was crushed, calcined, levigated, and subjected to every imaginable process. Bones, eggshells, seashells, chalk, clay, and even pearls were used. White chalk was widely used in the seventeenth and eighteenth centuries to provide one of the whitest whites. It can be used in distemper, but is not good as a pigment in oil, where it becomes almost transparent. Whiting, sometimes called Spanish white, is white chalk mixed with alum. When added to water to make whitening, it can be used, unbound, as a finish on raw plaster. If animal glue is added, it becomes soft distemper.

When limestone or chalk are heated, they make quicklime which, added to water, becomes slaked lime. Mixed with tar or lanolin, this becomes limewash, which can be tinted with earth pigments. White clays can be mixed in water to make a form of distemper; in oil they produce dirty off-whites.

Metals are the other main source of white pigments. White lead, or ceruse, was in production as early as the sixteenth century. Lead strips were hung above vinegar in an airtight barrel which was left for about eight weeks until the white pigment forming on the lead could be knocked off in flakes. The pigment was then left to bake in the sun. Lead white was the only white suitable for use in oils until the middle of the nineteenth century. Its main drawback was its toxicity, both for users and those involved in its manufacture.

Zinc oxide is one of the most used old white pigments, especially in its more concentrated form, Chinese white. Known from at least the sixteenth century, it was not until the late eighteenth century that it was considered for use as a pigment. In 1834 the firm of Winsor & Newton sold it under the name of Chinese white, by which it has remained known. Another white pigment, lithopone, first patented in 1874, was popular with decorators. Initially, lithopone darkened after being exposed to sunlight for only a day, but brightened again overnight. Such problems were eventually solved, and since the early years of this century, lithopone has been in regular use as a pigment for interior paints.

The world had to wait until the 1920s for the production of titanium white – the first reliable, permanent, non-toxic, bright white. Particularly successful as a watercolor and unaffected by light and heat, titanium white's good covering power has had a profound effect on the decorating trade.

Chalk has always been the most accessible white. It is soft and easily ground, and since it is for the most part free from impurities, it is easily converted to pigment.

A fascinating range of "old" whites is possible when you mix your own paints. The earth pigments give the best results. Raw umber added to white will give a coolish, neutral color. Black and yellow ocher mixed with white will give a similar tint. Burnt umber adds an earthy pinkiness, while burnt sienna creates an even pinker white. Yellow ocher nudges white toward cream.

White + yellow ocher

White + burnt sienna

White + yellow ocher + black

White + black

White + burnt umber

White + raw umber

ration

PREPARING TO PAINT

For a good, long-lasting paint finish on any surface, proper preparation is essential. This means achieving a surface that is sound, clean, dry, free of grease, and smooth. If necessary, call in a builder to deal with structural problems that may be causing cracks or condensation. Plastered walls that have previously been painted or papered may need stripping back to the original surface. Such preparation can seem to take a disproportionate amount of time, but years later, when the paint is still looking good, you will appreciate the hours put in at the beginning.

CLEARING THE ROOM

Start by clearing the room to give the maximum space to work in, using dropcloths to cover any furniture that cannot be moved. It is essential to plan carefully to avoid the possibility of, for instance, finding halfway through painting a wall on your own that you need an extra pair of hands to move a grand piano. Lift carpets or cover them in dropcloths, sticking a wide band of masking tape between the baseboard and carpet to prevent fluff from the carpet from getting in the paint. Remove light fixtures and door hardware. Light switches and electric sockets should be taken off or at least loosened. If you are not sure how to do this, employ a qualified electrician. Alternatively, cover switches and sockets with masking tape. For preparation and any plain painting on walls, work from a plank between two stepladders or between a stepladder and a small hop-up. When you need to work especially fast, as with fast-drying glazing coats, it is easier to use a single light stepladder that can be moved with one hand.

CLEANING THE SURFACE

The surfaces to be painted must be rendered clean, dry, and free of any flakes. Brush them to remove dust and cobwebs. Do not forget the top edges of doors, window frames, and architraves as well as the corners of panels and any recesses in moldings. Dust left in the crevices will find its way into a paint-filled brush and leave a dirty streak. How you clean the surfaces will depend on their finish and the paint you intend to use. If ceilings have been painted with soft distemper and you wish to repaint with latex, you should remove the soft distemper completely with hot water and a sponge. Similarly, you should never leave soft distemper on any surface that is to be recoated with an oil-bound distemper, as the new paint will certainly

crack and flake. If you intend to repaint with soft distemper, then just brushing away dust and cobwebs from the old distemper will usually be adequate. However, soft distemper is very absorbent, so if there is a heavy build-up or if you are planning a significant color change, it is best to remove most of it. For greasy or smoke-stained surfaces painted with oil-bound distemper, latex or flat-oil paint, wash with a solution of sugar soap. On other surfaces use a solution of mild detergent such as diluted dishwashing liquid. Make sure you rinse thoroughly.

Woodwork that has been stripped and then waxed provides very poor support for paint of any kind, inhibiting the drying of oil paint and repelling water paint. As much wax as possible should be removed, either by using a commercial paint or varnish stripper, or by rubbing with sandpaper, steel wool, and a cabinet scraper. Finish by washing with diluted detergent, rinsing, and allowing to dry; then coat with shellac to seal off any wax that may remain. Varnished woodwork that is still in good condition with few chips and scratches only needs a good sandpapering to provide a key. Badly chipped varnish should be stripped back to the bare wood.

REMOVING PAINT AND PAPER

Cornices and ceiling moldings often have a build-up of paint which obscures the details and should be removed. If the previous coats were of soft distemper, they should be laboriously cleaned with hot water and a toothbrush. Often a much-distempered molding will have been "sealed" with one or more coats of latex paint. These coats should be cleaned off by scoring the surface of the latex to allow the water to seep through to the soft distemper beneath. Once the latex paint has been completely removed, it is best to repaint with soft distemper which can later easily be washed off for future decoration. Steaming can be used, but is a job best left to a professional to avoid the risk of damage to the molding, which would be difficult to repair or replace.

Any paint technique benefits from careful preparation, but some are better suited to imperfect surfaces than others. The already broken surface of the handcut sponge block used to make the pattern shown here will absorb the unevenness of a lumpy wall. A hard rubber stamp, with its clearly defined edges, will not print well on a less-than-smooth surface.

Previously papered walls and ceilings should be approached with caution. Where the paper is in good condition, it can be painted over as long as the colors of the paper do not show through the new paint, but it is usually best to remove old wallpaper by soaking with water to which you have added a little detergent or special stripping fluid. Alternatively, use a steam stripper. When the paper is saturated, scrape it off. Vinyl papers can usually be peeled off, and any paper that remains can then be soaked with water and scraped off. If the paper has been varnished or painted, score through the top coat so that the water can penetrate and soften the paste. Once the paper has been removed, rinse off any residual paste. Always remove embossed or textured paper such as woodchip if you are planning a special paint effect.

SMOOTHING THE SURFACE

Fill any large holes or cracks, then sand the surfaces to give a smooth finish and to provide a key for subsequent coats. For large holes in woodwork, use a commercial wood putty, checking the label first to make sure that any primer you intend to use will adhere. Resin-based putty dries too hard for use with most water-based primers. Treat any knots in the wood with shellac-based knotting to prevent the resin from the knots seeping through and damaging the paint finish. Now sand the wood and apply a fine-surface putty where needed. This is especially useful to smooth out any prominent grain on new wood.

If old gloss paint has formed wrinkles, instead of removing the old paint completely, use a fine-surface putty to achieve a smooth surface, or sand down the old surface before applying the fine-surface putty. Take care when sanding woodwork as you may be rubbing off old lead-based paint, which is hazardous when inhaled. Sand using wet-and-dry paper moistened in a bucket of water, as any harmful dust will collect at the bottom of the bucket. Check with the local waste regulation authority before disposing of the dust, as it could pose a risk to other people.

Walls, woodwork and metalwork can now all be painted using water-based paints, with many obvious advantages, not least in drying times. Bathrooms tend to be humid places, so it is sensible to choose acrylics for the woodwork, and to finish the walls with a coat of acrylic varnish. There is even an acrylic-based paint system which allows you to paint metal items, such as sink supports, without stripping away all the rust beforehand.

On walls and ceilings scrape out any loose material from cracks and holes. Fill with a commercial putty, leaving it standing out from the wall surface, and let it dry before sanding flush. Feel the surface with your hand to locate any lumps, then use fine sandpaper wrapped around a sanding block, or wet-and-dry paper, to give a flat, smooth surface. Finally, brush any dust off the walls and paintwork and vacuum it off the floor to prevent it from billowing up and embedding itself in the new paint.

PRIMING THE SURFACE

As surfaces that have not previously been painted are very absorbent, the main consideration is to make sure that paint does not sink right in. New plaster or plasterboard that has been given a final skim coat of plaster is especially thirsty. To counteract this, prime the surface with a primer thinned with about ten percent water. This first coat will partially seal the surface and highlight any remaining imperfections. Deal with these, then sand them and apply a second, thicker coat of primer.

The type of paint you wish to use as a top coat will determine the primer. For a latex finish, prime with diluted latex. For oil-bound distemper, prime with diluted oil-bound distemper; and for soft distemper, use either diluted soft distemper or claircolle, the traditional primer for soft distemper. Shellac can also be applied as a primer on new plaster. It is a kind of varnish made from a naturally occurring resin (lac) thinned with alcohol. It penetrates well, dries fast, and is available in several forms, varying from dark to white. Use white shellac if the final color is to be white or pale. Dark shellac, even if applied very thinly, may need an extra top coat for complete coverage.

Acrylic primer is a strong, water-based primer that is useful for all final finishes. It is especially good over old oil-bound finishes such as gloss-painted woodwork that is to be repainted with a water-based paint. For new bare wood with a slightly rough surface, prime with sanding sealer before sanding. If the surface of the wood is smooth and has previously been painted, sand it after filling (see above), and prime with an acrylic primer. If the final coat is to be milk paint or oil-bound distemper, the first coat of paint will act as the primer and the second one as a top coat. It is worth noting that for the techniques and products described in this book, the use of a roller is not recommended. It gives a mottled, rather mechanical paint finish, whereas a brush produces a smoother, more deliberate look, and is more controllable.

ORDER OF PAINTING

Paint the ceiling first to avoid splashing freshly painted walls with ceiling paint. If the room has a molding, tackle this next. If you are right-handed, start in a right-hand corner and work toward the left; if left-handed, start in a left-hand corner. Paint the difficult bits first, for instance any elaborate molded decoration. Use a couple of small brushes of different sizes, and work along at least to the next corner before embarking on the simpler molded areas. Carefully cut in, or neatly paint along, the top edge where it meets the ceiling, with as few breaks as possible between sections of work. Next come the woodwork and walls, usually in that order, but it may suit your decorating project to give the woodwork a first coat, then the walls a first coat, followed by a second coat to the woodwork, and finishing with a second coat to the walls. By ending with the walls, you are able to cut in a good line between the walls and woodwork. There is no point (unless there is an enormous color difference) in trying to cut in the undercoats carefully. Indeed overlaps where woodwork meets wall will help provide a good basis for the last cut in. This cutting in is not as difficult as it might seem. A steady hand (steady breathing will help), a full enough brush (but not too full), and a little confidence are all that are needed.

When painting walls, work out from the windows, in strips running from top to bottom of the wall. The size of the strips will depend on the drying time of the paint you are using. The faster the paint dries, the narrower the strips should be to avoid the problems of seam lines. If you are painting paneled walls or a wall with a dado rail, deal with one edge at a time in order to achieve clean edges. For instance, on a wall with a dado rail, start with the wall above the rail. Next, paint the rail itself, cutting in a neat top edge to the rail where it meets the wall above, but do not worry too much about the area below the rail. Finally, paint below the rail, finishing the bottom edge of the rail as you go. When painting the baseboard, finish the bottom of the dado neatly. Apply the same sequence to paneled walls.

Breaking a room down to its elements can help organize the painting schedule. Finish the ceiling first. The top edge of the molding should be cut into the ceiling, but its bottom edge should overlap the walls. After painting the architraves, shelves, and doors, tackle the walls — which are cut into the edges of the woodwork, but overlap the baseboard. Finally, paint the top of the baseboard to make the bottom of the wall neat.

PREPARATION

PAINTING PANELED DOORS

When painting wood, always "lay off" the paint in the direction of the grain. On paneled doors, paint all the moldings first, without worrying about trying to achieve a neat edge at this early stage. Next paint the panels, cutting in to the edge of the moldings. Finally, paint the muntins (the vertical strips separating the panels), the horizontal rails, and then the vertical stiles or side pieces. When painting these sections, paint last those areas that finish off the ends of adjacent, previously painted areas. Therefore, on a door with two vertical panels top and bottom, deal first with the moldings and panels, then paint the two muntins separating the pairs of panels, followed by the three horizontal rails, and finish with the stiles at the side. Do not forget to paint the top edge of the door at the same time as the face of the top rail, both to get rid of the accumulated dirt and to avoid the build-up of paint that otherwise occurs at the arris, or the edge of the top rail. Finish by painting the top and the sides of the door frame.

PAINTING WINDOWS

Paint windows early in the day, leaving them open to dry until the end of the day when they can be closed. If you need to shut them sooner, wait until they are more than touch dry and lightly finger-dust the edges with talc or French chalk to prevent them from sticking. Start by painting the glazing bars – the strips of wood that separate the panes of glass. The sequence for painting the rest of the window – the rails and stiles – is the same as for painting paneled doors. In other words, finish by painting those sections that neaten the ends of previously painted areas. The final step is to paint the top and bottom bars of the frame, followed by the side bars and the windowsill. Where glass meets wood, the putty should be smooth and slightly rounded. Here the paint should be applied so that there is contact between the paint and the glass, but they barely touch. Once dry, remove any spots of paint from the glass with a razor blade in a holder.

For a sash window, work on the top sash first. This is to make sure that all of both sashes can be reached. Start by lowering the top sash and painting all of it, including the top rail. Raise the bottom sash to reach the lower part of the top sash. Then raise the painted top sash almost to the top of the window frame. Now raise the bottom sash slightly so that you can paint all of it, including the bottom rail. Finish by painting the top, bottom, and sides of the window frame and the windowsill.

PAINTING FURNITURE

The quality of preparation is even more important with small pieces of furniture which are subject to close scrutiny, wear, and tear. The principles are roughly the same as for woodwork and will depend on whether the furniture has been painted, polished, or varnished. Special cases are papier-mâché, cane, and bamboo. Papier-mâché should be treated just as wood, while bamboo and cane have very hard surfaces which should be sanded more carefully to ensure that the paint adheres. After sanding, treat them as wood. If old paint or varnish is in good condition, sand it with coarse-grit sandpaper followed by a finer grit. Fine fill, then prime. If the paint or varnish is rough and flaky, strip it all off with a commercial paint stripper, as large areas of wood putty applied to such a surface will most certainly get dislodged in time.

In stripping an old piece of furniture, original paint is sometimes revealed. If you think that there may be some original decoration behind the surface paint, do not use a paint stripper, which would remove the original, but instead scrape away with a knife or scalpel. If the decoration is in good condition, it can be touched up and revarnished. Alternatively, take color photographs and repaint. If the furniture has never been painted or varnished, sand it to remove any roughness. For a particularly fine finish, apply sanding sealer or size by brush, let it dry, then sand it again with fine sandpaper. Last, prime with acrylic primer. If you are going on to use milk paint, you can use a coat of diluted milk paint. Wicker, Lloyd Loom, and other similar furniture derive their strength from their flexibility. This can present difficulties when repainting because of the inflexibility of many paint finishes. Sand such surfaces as much as possible, then repaint using acrylic primer and acrylic top coats, which are more flexible.

For furniture that has been polished or waxed, remove the finish with a commercial stripper. Next rub it with fine steel wool, rinse with water, and finish by lightly rubbing with fine sandpaper before priming. When painting furniture, start with areas that are hidden, such as chair stretchers, and finish with those that will be most on show. For painting areas that are adjacent to one another, follow the rule about ending with those areas that finish off the ends of adjacent, previously painted areas.

White acrylic primer is a good all-purpose base coat for all paints. It is best applied as two thin coats rather than one thick one.

36

1

2

3

4

5

6

7

8

9

10

EQUIPMENT

LEFT A selection of brushes for all purposes. **1** Ordinary decorators' brushes in various sizes. On the whole, the longer the bristles, the smoother the finish. **2** Badger hair softener, invaluable in marbling and graining, but expensive. **3** Dusting brush for preparing surfaces, putting the figure in graining, and a possible substitute for a badger softener. **4** Artists' hogshair brushes, useful for mixing paints because they disperse stainers better than a stick. **5** Lining brushes for painting lines, details, and veins in marbling. **6** Stenciling brushes. Those with flexible bristles are best. **7** Hogshair glider, invaluable for finer textured work and graining. **8** Square-ended "one-stroke" watercolor brush for applying thin washes. **9** Artists' brushes for defining details. **10** Hogshair lining fitch, more useful for corners, edges, and inaccessible places than lining brushes.

BELOW Much of the equipment used for decorating – scissors, pencils, chalk, sponges, paper towels and masking tape, for example – can be found in any home. The more specialist items are identified below. **1** Stencil board. This is treated to make it water resistant, although it does become saturated after a while. It is best to cut two stencils at once so you can renew them easily. **2** Rubber stippler. Rubber is good if you want a coarse print. Hair stipplers give a more delicate finish, but are more expensive. **3** Steel graining combs, which come in sets. New ones may have to be sanded with an emery board to prevent scratching. **4** Wire brush for removing the soft part of the grain before pickling or distressing. **5** Line with chalk to be "snapped" against the wall to mark straight lines. **6** Steel wool. Invaluable in the early stages, but it will discolor finishes. **7** Paint bucket. Galvanized steel is best, although plastic is cheaper. Never trust the handle of a plastic bucket. **8** Foam sheet for cutting stamps. **9** Foam roller for applying paint to rubber or foam stamps. **10** Artists' palette and palette knife for mixing small quantities of paint. **11** Carpenter's level. Plastic is better than aluminum which marks walls. **12** Plumb line.

Diste

m p e r

Distemper – from the Italian *tempera*, meaning color blended with water – has been in common use for centuries. The name denotes a variety of paints in which washed and powdered chalk, usually known as whiting, is blended with water, a binder and pigment. Distempers were the chief household paints for walls, ceilings, and often woodwork until the emergence of plastic-based latex paint in the 1950s. For today's decorators, distemper has many advantages. Even when applied as a plain coat of paint, it produces an attractive flat, dry, chalky effect, with a more varied and less mechanical finish than that of latex paint.

Distempers are useful for both flat finishes and decorative paint techniques, providing a soft, understated finish that is very easy on the eye. They are inexpensive, give excellent coverage, and look particularly good as they age, making them especially suitable for old houses or cottages, or anywhere that a mellow effect is desirable. Another attraction of the paints is that they allow the wall beneath to "breathe", so they are especially appropriate for use in old buildings whose walls may be damp. Distemper can also be used on newly plastered walls, as it allows them to breathe, although they must be allowed to dry and harden thoroughly before coating. At the beginning of the nineteenth century, distemper was recommended as a stop-gap paint on newly built, freshly plastered walls that were later to be finished in oil paint. While the new masonry needed as long as a year to dry out completely, the plaster dried within about three months, when it could be covered with a coat of distemper.

Distempers, for years almost unobtainable, are now again available in a wide choice of colors varying from true pastel shades to vibrant hues, or as a basic white which can be mixed to the desired color. Distempers were traditionally colored with pure pigments, but commercially produced water stainers are often less expensive and allow more accurate color mixing. When coloring distemper it is helpful to know that it will dry much paler than its wet appearance. Use only a very little heat when drying samples; otherwise, the color will be distorted. There are three main types of distemper, soft, oil-bound, and limewash.

To produce the rich orange-red of these walls, apply two or three coats of distemper, each tinted a slightly different color. Start with a base coat of burnt sienna, yellow ocher, and pure red stainer and glaze over it with Venetian red or burnt sienna. The job can be done quickly, but allow each coat to harden properly before applying the next.

SOFT DISTEMPER

Soft distemper produces a beautiful but fragile finish that comes off easily to the touch and is not washable, so is not recommended for areas of heavy traffic. It is best suited to plain painting, simple colorwashing (see pp46-9), and sponging (pp50-51). Composed of whiting, size (animal glue), pigment, and water, it is sometimes also called size color or size distemper. Soft distemper has been made and used by theatrical scene painters for generations. There are many old recipes for soft distemper, and while their ingredients remain fairly constant, the proportions vary widely. The recipe below will quickly and easily produce enough distemper to paint the walls and ceiling of an average-sized room.

12lb/5.5kg whiting
¾lb/350g size powder
pigment

*Put the whiting in a large bucket, cover
with water, and let it soak for two or three hours.
After this time, pour off the excess water,
leaving a thick white paste. In another bucket,
mix the size powder with just enough water to soak.
After a few minutes, add 6pts/3l of boiling water,
and stir until the size powder is completely dissolved.
Let it cool slightly, then add the size to
the whiting paste. Mix thoroughly.
The result is white distemper which can be
colored as required. It should be used cold.*

Soft distemper can be strengthened with acrylic medium to reduce the fragility of its surface. The acrylic medium also reduces the distemper's covering power, but the addition of up to one part acrylic to seven parts distemper is acceptable. For the recipe above add 1¼pt/500ml. The binder is weakened when color is added, so when painting with soft distemper over soft distemper, if the base coat is any color other than white, it will be "woken up" by the top coat and will mix with the color of the top coat.

New coats of soft distemper can be applied over old coats provided there is not too much build-up and the color is the same or the base coat is white. If you regularly recoat with soft distemper, wash off the old coats every third time you recoat. When recoating with a different finish, especially with oil-bound distemper or latex, first completely remove the old soft distemper.

OIL-BOUND DISTEMPER

Despite its name, oil-bound distemper is a water-based paint. It is bound with size like soft distemper, but is strengthened with a small proportion of linseed oil. The combination of oil with water makes oil-bound distemper a type of primitive latex. Traditionally, it was mixed on site by adding oil to soft distemper. Nowadays, it is best to buy ready-made oil-bound distemper, because those produced commercially often have very complicated formulations which it would not be practical to reproduce at home.

Oil-bound distemper is slightly less permeable than soft distemper, giving a washable finish for use in situations where soft distemper would be unsuitable, such as kitchens and bathrooms. For priming new surfaces, use a diluted coat of oil-bound distemper, leaving it to dry before applying the full coat. Unlike soft distemper, some oil-bound distempers can be used on outside walls, where the paint's surface gradually disintegrates and discolors in an attractive way.

Colorwashing and sponging with oil-bound distemper can give a richer effect than with soft distemper: the underlying coats will not be "woken up" by the addition of top coats, so lighter colors can be used over darker base coats to build up successive layers of washes. However, when oil-bound distemper is mixed with a high proportion of water stainers or pigment, the binder can be weakened. In such cases, acrylic medium can be used to counteract this effect. Oil-bound distemper is very effective for freestyle painting (see pp66-9), spattering (pp52-3) and stamping with a piece of cut sponge (pp62-5). Oil-bound distemper can also be used for simulating stone (pp54-7) and marbling (pp58-61).

LIMEWASH

Limewash is a type of distemper which has been used for many centuries to paint brickwork, plastered surfaces, and woodwork in stables, sheds, basements, workshops, and factories.

The term limewashing is often erroneously used to mean white-washing, although limewash is an entirely different paint. In effect, limewashing coats surfaces with a thin but durable layer of lime. Limewash is made in the same way as soft distemper except that slaked lime is used as the binder rather than whiting. When slaked lime is added to water, it bubbles and gives off a great deal of heat, producing a highly caustic mixture, so limewashing should only be undertaken by experienced professionals. Limewash can be tricky to use; it requires constant stirring, will not adhere to surfaces with which it is chemically incompatible, and can be tinted only with "lime-friendly" pigments. Once it has been applied, it needs as much ventilation as possible to help it dry quickly. Limewash is used the world over, often annually as part of "spring cleaning" as it is renowned for its disinfecting properties and can easily be recoated.

LEFT *When this eighteenth-century fisherman's house on the French Côte d'Azur was renovated, the original paint finishes were uncovered. The stone staircase is complemented by walls colorwashed in shades of blue-green distemper.*

RIGHT *Oil-bound distemper is better than soft distemper for humid rooms. Although soft distemper can be used, it needs to be recoated very frequently because of its fragile nature. Here, decorative glazed tiles take the wear around the bath where distemper might have been washed away.*

Colorwashing

Soft and oil-bound distemper can be used to great effect in simple colorwashing, as can be seen in the samples shown overleaf. However, subsequent coats of soft distemper will "wake up" earlier coats. Soft distemper is strongest when it is used in its natural white state. Adding colorants weakens the finish, so colored distemper will, if used as a base coat for a colorwashed finish, pick up and mix with the wash coat. When using soft distemper as a base coat, it is best to use it uncolored, not to use strongly contrasting wash coats, and not overwork the top coat application.

If strong contrasts or a colored base coat are wanted, it is best to use an oil-bound distemper for the base coat, because it remains stable beneath successive coats of paint. The base coat should be diluted with water to the consistency of thin milk. Soft or oil-bound distemper can be applied over the top of this base. Distemper can also be applied over walls painted with latex.

Whichever coat is applied last will provide the dominant color in the room.

a

TOOLS AND EQUIPMENT
Soft or oil-bound distemper Pigments or stainers Large decorators' brush Coarse decorators' brush
Level of skill required Simple **Recommended on** Smooth or uneven wall surfaces

OPPOSITE *To achieve a rich finish like this use a lime yellow wash over a base coat of white tinted with yellow ocher and a little burnt sienna, burnt umber and lime yellow.*

Base coat
Using the large decorators' brush, apply two coats of base color. Let it dry overnight.

Applying the wash coat
Use the coarse brush to apply the wash quickly with a loose crisscross motion, leaving definite brush marks (**a** and **b**). This movement means the diluted paint is less likely to drip. Work in blocks, moving from the top to the bottom of the wall. You will need to work quickly as the paint dries fast. Be sure to brush from dry paint into wet, as brushing from wet into dry gouges holes in the wet paint. Let the first coat dry before applying subsequent coats.

b

DISTEMPER

Base coat
White soft distemper

Base coat
White oil-bound distemper tinted
with black and blue

Base coat
White oil-bound distemper tinted
with black and blue

Wash coat
White soft distemper tinted with
blue and raw umber and diluted
with water

Wash coat
White oil-bound distemper tinted
with blue and raw umber and
diluted with water

Wash coat
White oil-bound distemper tinted
with more black and blue and
diluted with water

COLORWASHING

Base coat
White oil-bound distemper tinted
with raw umber, yellow ocher
and burnt umber

Base coat
White oil-bound distemper tinted
with black, raw umber, and
yellow ocher

Base coat
White oil-bound distemper tinted with yellow
ocher and small quantities of burnt sienna,
burnt umber, and lime yellow

Wash coat
Base coat mixed with more white
oil-bound distemper and diluted
with water

Wash coat
White oil-bound distemper tinted
with burnt sienna, yellow ocher
and red, and diluted with water

Wash coat
White oil-bound distemper tinted
with lime yellow and diluted
with water

Sponging

Sponging has been a popular finish for a century or more. It used to be employed to imitate marble and granite. In the 1920s and 1930s, it was used in much the same way as today – to introduce a second color over an existing background, but as an imaginative finish rather than as a precise imitation of a particular stone. At that time, sponging was often arranged in panels on the wall, with surrounding areas left plain. This proved to be an excellent way of avoiding the difficulty of achieving a good print in the corners of a room and toward the upper and lower edges of a wall. Another way of overcoming the problem is to hold a piece of cardboard against the ceiling or edges of the wall where you do not want the sponge to print, and to cut a small wedge-shaped piece of sponge to use in the corners. The finish in sponging can be dense or open. It should always be even, and the shape of the sponge should never be apparent in the finished decoration.

TOOLS AND EQUIPMENT

Base coat
White soft distemper

First sponged coat	**Second sponged coat**
White soft distemper tinted with yellow ocher, yellow, and blue, and diluted with water to the consistency of light cream	The same mix as for the first sponged coat, but with slightly less blue. Mix this coat first, then add more blue to one half of the paint to make first coat

Large decorators' brush
Natural sponge
Board for testing technique

Level of skill required Simple
Recommended on Smooth or rough wall surfaces

Base coat
Using a large decorators' brush, apply two coats of white distemper to create a flat finish. Let it dry.

Filling the sponge
Wet a large natural sponge with water and squeeze it out completely. Then wet it well with the paint mixture and squeeze it out again (**a**). The sponge should be almost dry and not overloaded with paint. Test on a board for consistency and to try out the technique before moving on to the wall.

a

b

c

Applying the first coat
Apply the paint using a light, dabbing touch, never dwelling too long on one particular area, and constantly changing the angle of the wrist to vary the pattern (**b** and **c**).

Fill the sponge whenever necessary, taking particular care to squeeze out excess paint each time. Test on the board for consistency of coverage before returning to the wall. Allow the first coat to dry before applying the second.

Applying the second coat
Sponge on the second coat in the same way (**d**).

d

Spattering

Spattering seems to have been introduced in the late eighteenth century as a way of imitating the stone porphyry. Its decorative possibilities are similar to sponging – edges and corners are difficult to handle and curved surfaces well nigh impossible. As with sponging, the effect can be dense or open, but should always be regular enough to disguise the pattern given by a single brush-load. Test first on a piece of board to make sure the diluted paint does not run and that the technique has been mastered before starting work. Spattering is messy, so make sure the areas that are not being spattered are well covered.

TOOLS AND EQUIPMENT

Base coat
White oil-bound distemper tinted with red, burnt sienna, and yellow ocher

First spatter coat
White oil-bound distemper tinted with blue and raw umber and diluted with water to the consistency of light cream

Second spatter coat
White oil-bound distemper tinted with black, diluted with water to the consistency of thin cream and strengthened with 20 percent acrylic medium

Third spatter coat
White oil-bound distemper diluted with water to the consistency of light cream

Large decorators' brush
1½in/40mm brush
Stick
Board for testing technique

Level of skill required Simple
Recommended on Smooth or rough surfaces
Not suitable for Curved surfaces and moldings

Base coat
Apply two or more coats of the base color with the large decorators' brush to create a flat finish.

Spattering
Dip the 1½in/40mm brush into the first spatter coat and, holding it over the paint pot, roll the brush handle between the palms of your hands (known as wringing). Excess paint will be spun off and that which remains will be left in the tips of the bristles. If the brush is overloaded, the spatters will be too heavy. Holding the brush about 12in/30cm away from the surface to be decorated, apply the first spatter coat by hitting the stock of the paint-loaded brush sharply against a stick (**a** and **b**). Make sure the spatters are evenly spaced.

c

d

a

e

b

Building up the layers
When the first layer (**c**) is complete, apply the second spatter color, again ensuring that the spatters are evenly spaced (**d**). The high proportion of pigment or water stainers to oil-bound distemper in this mix weakens the binder, so acrylic medium is added to counteract this effect. Test first to make sure the paint does not run.

Repeat with the third, white spatter coat (**e**).

TOOLS AND EQUIPMENT

Base coat
White oil-bound distemper tinted with
raw umber

Block color
Base coat tinted with additional raw umber
diluted with water to the consistency of
light cream

Joint line color
Block color tinted with black

Large decorators' brush
Soft pencil
Straightedge
Carpenter's level
Fitch (small decorators' brush)
3in/70mm brush
Medium lining brush

Level of skill required
Intermediate
Recommended on
Smooth wall surfaces

Trompe l'oeil stone blocks

As pattern to break up uninterrupted areas of blank wall, fake stone blocks and even painted brickwork have been used for centuries. They evoke the romantic effect of stone walls with none of their inconvenience and are especially suitable for halls where the "natural" material links inside with outside, and any other area where a hard material seems appropriate. The principles of simple trompe l'oeil painting are easily grasped, and the effect works best on a limited area. It is important to be consistent with the imagined light source.

In this room painted stone walls complement a real stone chimney-piece. The success of the effect depends upon the careful choice of earth colors that match the stone and the appropriately dry finish produced by distemper. Trompe l'oeil need not aspire to grand illusions. Playing with the surface of a wall and adding cracks and chips that do not immediately strike the eye is usually more acceptable in smaller rooms. Such details as the lizard running down the wall toward the door (above) should only be attempted by the highly skilled.

DISTEMPER

Base coat

Using the decorators' brush, apply two or more coats of the base color to create a flat finish.

Marking out the blocks

Using a soft pencil, straightedge, and level, mark out the blocks (**a**). Start with the horizontal lines before adding the vertical ones. The size of the blocks should be in proportion to the wall, with each one approximately twice as long as it is deep.

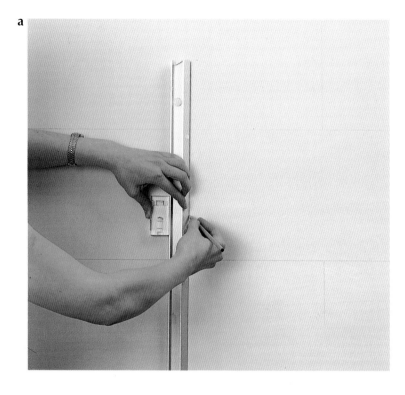

Painting the blocks

Use the fitch to paint the edges of the blocks first (**b**), then paint the area inside the marked blocks using the 3in/70mm brush (**c**). Apply the paint in bands running roughly parallel to the long side of the block, leaving a small gap between blocks. Vary the pressure on the brush and with it the amount of paint applied, to achieve a finished effect which mimics the strata in natural stone.

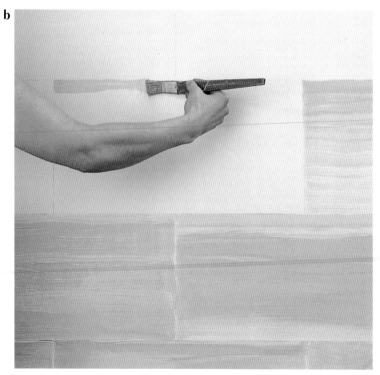

Adding the ripples

Use a dry fitch on the wet paint to add slight modifications, such as ripples, to the strata (**d**).

Painting the joint lines

Hold a straightedge beside each horizontal pencil line and, using a medium lining brush, paint the joint lines one block at a time. This will give the finished wall a natural, uneven look. Use the straightedge as a guide for the hand only; if the brush is used directly against the straightedge, paint will seep underneath. The color used for painting the joint lines can be off-white so that it resembles mortar, or dark so that the lines look like a shadow, as shown here. The important thing to remember is that the finished wall should not be overwhelmed by an over-insistent pattern of joints.

Repeat for the vertical lines (**e** and **f**).

Marbling

Before starting to marble, try to look at marble samples or color photographs of marble to become familiar with its main characteristics – its translucency, how the veins run through the stone, and the way the secondary veins form a crisscross pattern. Afterward, put these sources of inspiration to one side. Trying to copy exactly can result in a stilted and disappointing parody. Because oil-bound distemper can never be thinned to a completely translucent glaze, the marbling shown here creates an impression rather than a realistic reproduction of marble.

This type of marbling looks good in spaces like halls and dining rooms, but acrylics may be a better choice than distemper for marbling bathrooms, where condensation could be a problem (see pp154-5). Variety and interest can be added by breaking the marble surface up into imitation blocks.

In a Venetian hall, trompe l'oeil marbling in distemper has been used to create the illusion of several marbles of different colors set in panels.

TOOLS AND EQUIPMENT

Base coat
White oil-bound distemper

First color
White oil-bound distemper tinted with blue and raw umber and diluted with water to the consistency of light cream

Second color
First color mixed with additional white oil-bound distemper and diluted with water to the consistency of light cream

Vein color
First color tinted with very little black and diluted with water mixed to the consistency of light cream

Large decorators' brush
1in/25mm brush
1½in/40mm brush
Dusting brush or badger softener
Pointed No. 12 artists' brush

Level of skill required Intermediate
Recommended on
Smooth wall surfaces

a

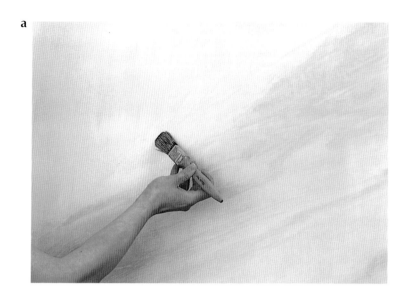

c

b

d

Base coat
Apply two or more coats of the base color with a large decorators' brush to create a flat finish.

Painting the bands of color
Applying the first color with the 1in/25mm brush and the second with the 1½in/40mm brush, paint roughly diagonal bands of alternating color (**a** and **b**). Use a dry dusting brush or badger softener to soften the areas between the colors while the paint is still wet.

Painting the veins
Apply the vein color with a pointed No. 12 artists' brush. The veins should roughly follow the diagonals (**c** and **d**).

It is possible to create the impression of marble blocks on a wall, marking it in the same way as you would stone blocks (see pp54-7). In this case, alternate the direction of the diagonal grain of the marbling with each block.

Because of its directness, marbling in distemper will produce a simple, understated effect where the elaboration of richer techniques might be inappropriate. The proportion of veining to background here is nicely judged.

TOOLS AND EQUIPMENT

Base coat
White oil-bound distemper tinted with blue, black, and burnt umber

Paint for first stage of stamping
Base coat mixed with more white oil-bound distemper

Paint for second stage of stamping
Base coat tinted with blue and burnt umber plus a little black

Paper
Craft knife or scalpel
Firm-textured sponge
Chalk or soft pencil
Cutting mat or heavy cardboard
Glue
Large decorators' brush
Straightedge
Carpenter's level
Piece of glass or formica
Small foam roller
Board for testing technique
½in/12mm brush

Level of skill required Advanced
Recommended on Smooth wall surfaces

Two-stage sponge stamping

Stamping with sponge-cuts is a way of producing an effect very like wallpaper, with the added advantages of flexibility of design and color. The pattern should not consciously betray its origins – the effect to aim for is that of a good hand-printed wallpaper, with all its inevitable minor irregularities. The design is a quatrefoil, with the first stamp forming the basic shape and the second picking out its edges, contributing to a three-dimensional effect.

a

Drawing the first stamp
Draw the quatrefoil design onto paper and cut around the edges using a craft knife or scalpel (**a**). Using either chalk or pencil depending on the color of the sponge, draw around the edges of the paper to transfer the shape to the sponge (**b**). The motif used here is 2½in/65mm wide and 3½in/90mm deep.

b

c

e

Drawing and cutting the second stamp

Draw the quatrefoil design onto a second piece of sponge and copy freestyle the areas which you wish to print as the shadow effect (**e**). Using a scalpel, cut away the excess sponge as before with vertical and horizontal cuts to leave small raised areas which will print as shadow. The second stamping will overprint part of the first.

d

f

Cutting the first stamp

Cut around the chalk line, cutting downward at a slight angle toward the outer edge through half the thickness of the sponge (**c**). Make a second horizontal cut in from the edge as far as the first vertical cut, and cut right around the sponge so the design stands away from the base of the sponge like a step or plateau with slightly sloping sides (**d**). The slope, or batter, gives strength to the block and means pressure is transferred evenly to the sides of the stamp when it is used.

Making handles

Glue some scraps to the back of both stamps to form handles (**f**).

Base coat

Using the decorators' brush, apply two or more coats of the base color to the surface to create a flat finish.

Plotting the design

When the base coat is dry, lightly draw a regular grid on the wall using chalk, a tape measure, straightedge, and level (**g**). The grid used here was 4in/10cm square, but the dimensions can be varied to suit the proportions of your room. The stamp should be centered on each intersection. Since the purpose of the grid is simply to plot the positions of each motif, rub out the chalk lines, leaving only the crosses at the intersections.

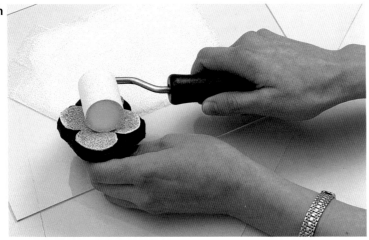

Loading the first stamp

Put a small quantity of the first color onto a smooth, firm, non-absorbent surface such as glass or a piece of formica. Use a small foam roller to apply a thin layer of paint to the first sponge stamp (**h**). The roller ensures that the paint is applied evenly over the surface of the stamp.

Sponging the first color

Stamp the design on the wall in the marked positions. Apply even pressure to ensure the paint is transferred to the wall uniformly (**i** and **j**). It is a good idea to practice first on a piece of board held in an upright position. Reapply paint to the stamp after each print.

Touching up

When the paint is dry, use the ½in/12mm brush, lightly loaded with paint and with its hairs splayed out, to stipple extra paint onto any areas where uneven pressure has left a gap in the print (**k**).

Sponging the second color

When the first color is completely dry, fill the second stamp as before with the darker second color. Print on top of the quatrefoil design, judging the position by eye (**l**).

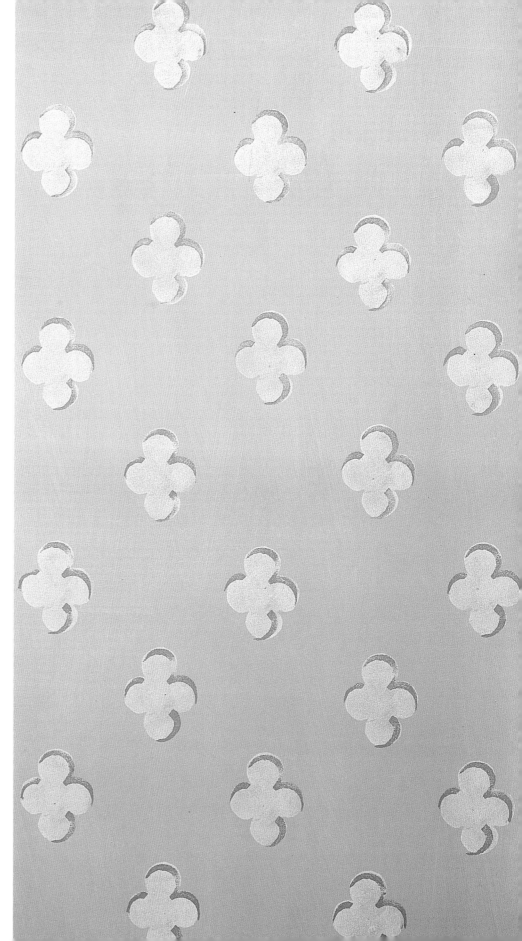

TOOLS AND EQUIPMENT

Base coat
White oil-bound distemper

Gray colorwash
White oil-bound distemper
tinted with black and raw umber
and diluted with water to the
consistency of thin milk

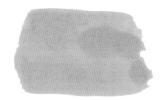

Yellow colorwash
White oil-bound distemper
tinted with lemon yellow, yellow
ocher, and a little red and blue,
and diluted with water to the
consistency of thin milk

Main color for the garland
White oil-bound distemper
tinted with yellow ocher and
burnt sienna and diluted with
water to the consistency
of light cream

Shading color for the garland
Main color tinted with
additional burnt sienna and
a little burnt umber

Large decorators' brush
Soft pencil or chalk
Straightedge
Carpenter's level
Chalk line (optional)
Medium lining brush
No. 10 artists' watercolor brush
Fine sandpaper (optional)

Level of skill required Advanced
Recommended on Smooth wall surfaces

Freestyle painted garland

Garlands of various sorts have always been a favorite form of decoration. In Pompeii they were frequently painted both naturalistically and in a fairly abstract manner. The enriched parts of the entablatures of Roman temples and other buildings are often carved as garlands and were no doubt painted where they were not carved.

In this design the comparatively strong color and eye-catching rhythm of the bay garland acts as a decorative link between two colors. The design would probably work best as a dado, where the upper wall painted pale gray meets the yellow lower wall. It would also look good at the top of a wall with the pale gray of the ceiling coming down to meet the yellow wall at the frieze of leaves.

a

Colorwashing the wall
Use the large decorators' brush to paint the entire wall with the white base coat, then colorwash it in gray following the instructions on p46 (**a**).

Marking the center line

To mark the line for the border design, whether you are using it as a dado or a frieze, measure the required height at points along the wall with a straightedge and level. Mark these points in soft pencil, then join the marks using a pencil and a straightedge (**b**). Alternatively, snap a chalk line across the wall. This is a length of string coated with chalk which provides an accurate way of marking lines.

Colorwash below the line using the yellow wash (**c**). The addition of red and blue to this wash (giving purple, the complementary of yellow) has the effect of muting the otherwise vivid yellow.

b

c

d

Marking out the freestyle design

Measure along, above, and below the pencil or chalk line to mark the position of the twining stems (**d**). The stem in this design crosses the line at 9in/23cm intervals and alternately rises and falls 1in/25mm above and 1in/25mm below the line halfway between each crossing point.

Start by marking with a dot the points at 9in/ 23cm intervals where the stem will cross the line. Halfway between these points, 4½in /11.5cm from each, mark another set of points approximately 1in/25mm alternately above and below the line. These points mark the highest and lowest limits of the curve. Using a pencil, carefully and lightly join the dots to make the snaking line.

Painting the stem, leaves, and berries
Using a medium lining brush, paint the stem in the main color following the wavy line. Take care at the beginning and end of each brush stroke to make sure there is no excess paint at these points.

With a No. 10 artists' watercolor brush, paint on the leaves and berries (**e** and **f**), using the illustration of the completed design opposite as a guide. Each leaf and berry should be executed with a single brushstroke. At the start of each brushstroke, the hairs of the brush should taper to a fine point. As the stroke is extended, apply gentle pressure to spread the hairs, then release the pressure to bring them to a point again. Recharge the brush and bring it to a point for each and every stroke.

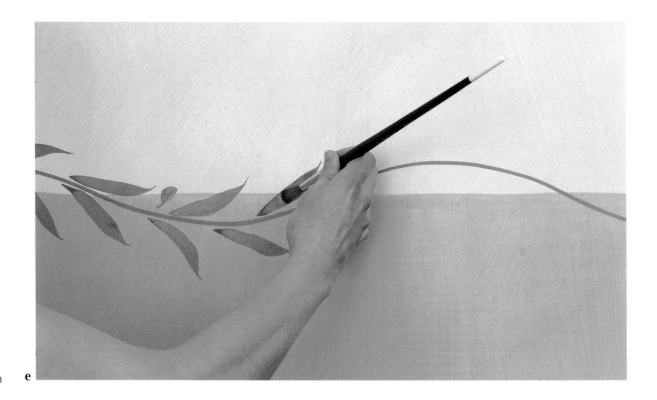

e

f

Painting the shading

With the same size brush and employing the same technique, apply the shading color to half of each leaf and each berry (**g**). This stage of the painting provides a good opportunity to thicken any leaves that look a little narrow.

Refining the finish

For a "distressed" look, rub the wall gently with fine sandpaper when all the paint is completely dry (**h**).

Milk paints add another dimension to the distemper family as they are washable, offer a ready-mixed palette of rich dark colors, and give a durable finish to woodwork. Just as egg was used in Renaissance tempera painting to fix or bind the pigment to the surface to be decorated, so milk – another staple of the kitchen – was enlisted for the same purpose.

The exact ingredient used was, and still is, casein – the thick curd that separates from the whey when milk has been left to sour. The curd was washed, dried, and ground, then mixed with some fresh slaked lime (acting as a disinfectant) and with a large quantity of pure pigment, hence the strong palette of milk paint colors.

Although milk paints were used for decoration by the ancient Egyptians, Greeks, and Romans, as well as by later Europeans, these paints are now mostly associated with the interiors of Colonial America. Before about 1725, oil paints were seldom used in America as they were expensive to make and there was no reliable source of the necessary linseed oil. Limewashes (see p44), distempers (p42), and milk paints, however, could be produced more easily.

While limewashes were excellent for painting plaster and stonework, distemper, which was used for interior walls, had a tendency to rub off. Milk paint answered the need for an economical, durable paint which would be especially suitable for painting wooden paneling and woodwork.

Ingredients were easy to obtain: skimmed milk came from the farmer as a byproduct of cheese- and butter-making. Lump lime came from the general store, while most communities had a "paint mine" containing iron oxide which provided a warm earth-colored pigment. A blue-green pigment was probably the result of mixing potash and green earth, containing copper carbonate. Early nineteenth-century recipes for milk paint also sometimes included linseed, nut, or caraway oil.

The resulting paint was very versatile. It dried without a shine, giving a finish similar to that of oil-bound distemper. It penetrated the pores of the wood so that after a few weeks it became a tough, washable film. Milk paint could be used for plain painting of plaster or stone; it could be thinned with water to make a glaze, or used in a thicker consistency for freestyle painting or stenciling.

Historical recipes are too complex for the modern decorator to attempt to re-create. If you wish to create your own colors, however, commercially produced white milk paint can be tinted with water stainers, gouache, and powder pigments, but not with acrylics. In any case, ready-colored milk paint is widely available in powder form or ready-mixed. They offer an unusual selection of colors which often reflect their Colonial origins; and in addition to bonding well to many different surfaces, milk paints dry fast, smell pleasant during use, and are non-toxic, making it possible to breathe comfortably and even sleep on the same day in a room just painted. As with other paints in this book, milk paints are water-soluble, allowing brushes to be easily cleaned without harmful solvents. However, as the casein is such a strong binder, the paint should not be allowed to dry hard in the bristles, as it will then be impossible to remove. It would also be unwise to use milk paint on its own in conditions of extreme dampness or humidity because the protein may encourage the growth of mildew. You could, however, get around this problem by coating the paint with a final layer of acrylic varnish to seal the surface.

Milk paints are a complete paint system in themselves, so new, previously unpainted surfaces need no priming. If you are painting on new plaster, make sure that it has been allowed to dry and harden thoroughly before applying a first coat of milk paint diluted with water to penetrate and seal the surface. When recoating, old milk paint need not be removed first, but can be sanded and painted over. In addition to giving an attractive surface in plain painting, milk paints, because of their strong colors, are an excellent choice for stenciling (see pp80-89), block printing (pp78-9), and freestyle painting (pp90-93).

If you are buying milk paints in powder form, they will need to be diluted with water to the required consistency. The amount of water will vary from job to job and will also be affected by temperature and humidity. It is a question of trial and error, although all suppliers provide an indication of the most usual dilution rates. For glazing work, large quantities of water can be added to achieve the slightest suggestion of color. For stenciling and freestyle work, add less water for a thicker mix. Milk paint has a naturally tough finish, but wax, oil, or varnish can be used as a finishing coat to provide extra protection for surfaces that are subject to a lot of wear and tear.

Different manufacturers produce milk paints with varying formulations, but they are all fast-drying, and most will be dry enough to apply a second coat after about four hours.

Using the fairly limited palette of pigments at their disposal in a simple milk binder, the decorators of Colonial America were able to create richly patterned environments using a handful of stencils, as seen in this room in the Shelburne Museum, Vermont.

Milk paints are ideal for painting on wood, and their toughness makes them suitable for areas such as kitchens. Rich in pigments, they come in a choice of colors that lend themselves to both historic and modern interiors. The saturated color and silky finish of the paint applied to the broad wooden planks in an old American kitchen imparts a gentle glow to the room (above), while the pale blue milk paint which has been rubbed down to produce a distressed finish on the cabinets of a simple kitchen (right) has a calm, timeless quality.

Flat painting

The tough washable finish of milk paints makes them ideal for woodwork in heavily used areas, such as kitchens. Traditional milk paints are available in ready-colored powders, and most of the colors are based on research into those used in American historic buildings and antique furniture. The colors are all very much earth-based and rich in pigments, but can like any other paint be tinted and altered. Here a ready-colored powdered milk paint is used on a row of kitchen pegs. It is very important to follow the instructions given below for mixing the powder to ensure a smooth consistency.

Mixing milk paints from powder makes them extremely versatile and economical, since their consistency can be accurately tailored to the job. For example, stenciling – for which milk paint is ideal – requires a much stiffer mix than plain painting.

TOOLS AND EQUIPMENT

Sea-green milk paint in powder form
1in/25mm decorators' brush
Danish oil

Level of skill required Simple
Recommended on All surfaces

a

b

Mixing the paint
Measure equal quantities of milk paint powder and warm water into separate containers. Gradually add the powder to the water (**a**) and mix very thoroughly – a kitchen blender is ideal for this. Leave the paint to stand for 10-15 minutes, until it thickens slightly. Add a little more warm water if needed. A mixture the consistency of light cream is usually best for flat painting, although this may vary according to the porosity of the surface to be painted.

Applying the paint
Using the 1in/25mm brush, apply the first coat evenly (**b**). For most woods, no primer is necessary as the first coat acts as a primer, but close-grained hardwoods such as maple or birch may require a special milk paint primer. Leave to dry. If required, sand the first coat lightly with fine sandpaper, then apply a second coat.

Finishing touches
For a lustrous finish, once the second coat is completely dry, brush on a coat of Danish oil. In addition to giving a shine, this adds protection where there will be a lot of wear and tear. Other accessories such as plate racks can be painted to match.

Rubber stamping

Milk paint is ideal for rubber stamping, since it can be mixed to a thick consistency and will dry quickly and evenly. It can be stamped onto any base other than soft distemper, where there is a risk of the stronger milk paint pulling away the weaker base coat. Rubber stamps are difficult to cut, so this project uses two that can be bought ready-made. If you are using powdered milk paint, mix all the white paint required first before dividing it up and tinting with stainers. Because so little paint is needed for the stamping, it makes economic sense to tint white milk paint for all the colors required.

TOOLS AND EQUIPMENT

Base coat
White milk paint tinted
with yellow ocher,
lime yellow, raw umber,
and burnt sienna, then diluted
with water to the
consistency of light cream

First stamp color
White milk paint tinted with blue
and burnt sienna

Second stamp color
White milk paint

Finishing coat (optional)
Flat acrylic varnish

Large decorators' brush
Chalk
Soft pencil
Straightedge
Carpenter's level
Piece of glass or formica
Small foam roller
Ready-made rubber stamps
Cardboard for testing technique

Level of skill required
Intermediate
Recommended on
Smooth wall surfaces

Preparing the wall
Paint the background a solid color in the base coat, using the decorators' brush. Plot the positions for the stamps using the grid method described on page 64, marking the positions of the white stamps with chalk and those of the blue stamps with light pencil.

Preparing the stamps
Put some of the first stamp color on a smooth flat surface such as a piece of glass or formica and use a small foam roller to apply the paint evenly to the rubber stamp (**a**).

a

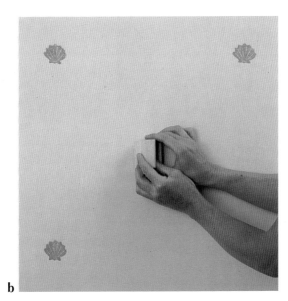
b

c

Stamping the shells and starfish
Stamp the shell design on the wall by positioning each stamp centrally over its pencil mark (**b**). It is wise to practice using the stamp on cardboard first, only printing the wall itself once the technique has been mastered. After printing all the shells, use the white milk paint to print the starfish motif on the positions marked out in chalk (**c**).

Finishing coat
If you are painting a particularly humid bathroom, apply a coat of flat acrylic varnish to seal the wall and discourage mildew.

Stenciling on walls

This design is based on an early nineteenth-century American wall stencil. Although similar work was done elsewhere, it is usually in the United States that we find the best preserved and documented examples. The decorator of around 1820 would have re-used a set of stencils (cut in leather, metal, or heavy cardboard) over and over again, in new combinations and with the spacing altered to fit the proportions of the walls. Arranged in vertical bands, the pattern uses two two-color stencils and one single-color stencil. Simpler designs can be used, of course, but the principles remain the same. To re-create this design, trace the stencils shown on page 82 and scale them up on a photocopier to the required size. Alternatively, you could devise your own design by tracing from a book or photograph.

A nineteenth-century American wall stencil with bands of alternating motifs picked out in red and green provided the general inspiration for this design.

TOOLS AND EQUIPMENT

Base coat
White milk paint tinted with burnt sienna, yellow ocher and red

First stencil color
Green milk paint

Second stencil color
Scarlet milk paint tinted with a little blue

Tracing paper
Soft pencil
Carbon paper
Stencil board
Craft knife or scalpel
Cutting mat or heavy cardboard
Large decorators' brush
Graph paper
Straightedge
Carpenter's level
Old knife or 1in/25mm brush
Palette, old plate, or jar lid
Stencil brush
Lint-free cloth
Masking tape

Level of skill required Advanced
Recommended on Smooth wall surfaces

80

The five stencils used in this room were adapted from a design reproduced in a book on Colonial decoration. You could produce your own patterns by tracing a design from a book and scaling it up on a photocopier.

A

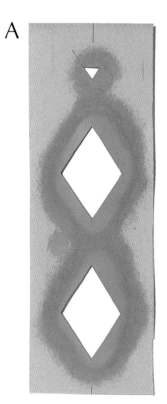

B

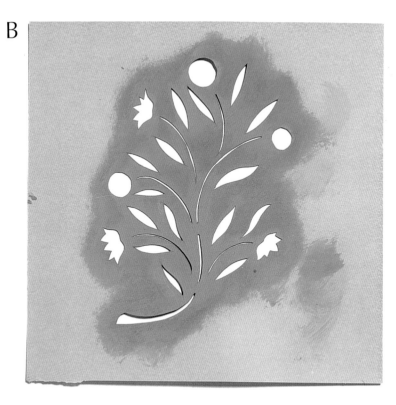

C

D

E

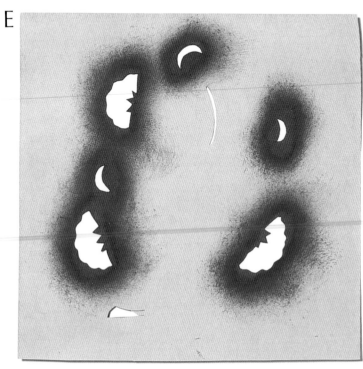

Tracing and cutting the stencils

Use a photocopier to scale up the stencil designs to fit your grid. This project uses the stencils reproduced opposite, but you could trace your own patterns from a book using tracing paper (**a**). Using carbon paper, transfer the designs to appropriately sized pieces of stencil board (**b**). Use a craft knife or scalpel on a cutting mat or piece of heavy cardboard to cut out the stencils (**c**).

Base coat

Paint the base coat to a solid color using the decorators' brush.

Planning the grid

When stenciling a whole room, first decide which is the dominant or most visible wall. This may be the wall facing the door, or one containing a chimney. Using graph paper, work out how many times the vertical lines of diamonds in the finished design (see p82) should appear on the wall, and from this, calculate how far apart the vertical lines should be. Unless the room is square, the spacing may not fit the other two walls. You may be left with an incomplete pattern in the corners unless minor adjustments are made to the spacing by widening or narrowing it at regular intervals.

Marking the grid

Mark the vertical lines lightly on the wall with a pencil, straightedge, and level. If the stencils do not exactly fit the height of the wall, it is usually best to have complete stencils at the top and incomplete patterns at dado or floor level.

Starting at the top of the wall, draw in the horizontal lines the same distance apart as the vertical lines to create a grid. Halfway between each vertical line, mark a point on each horizontal line. To prevent excess pencil marks on the finished wall, erase the horizontal lines except at the points where they cross the verticals. These crosses are for centering stencils **B, C,** and **E**.

a

b

c

First stencil color

With an old knife or small brush, dab a little of the green milk paint onto a palette, old plate, or jar lid and fill the stencil brush with the paint, working it well into the bristles. Be sparing with the paint, as an overloaded brush will result in the excess seeping behind the stencil. Practice first on spare cardboard or paper by brushing in a roughly circular motion or by pouncing (using a dabbing motion). As the effects are different in each case, it is wise to experiment with these two techniques first.

Stencil A: Diamond

Working from the top down, hold stencil **A** on the vertical line, and apply the paint (**d**). Since this is a small stencil which can easily be held by hand, there is no need to use masking tape to hold it in position. The small triangle at the top of stencil **A** shows where to position the stencil relative to the diamond above. If any paint gets onto the back of the stencil, wipe it off with a lint-free cloth. Complete all the prints from each stencil before starting the next (**e**).

Stencil B: Posy

Position stencil **B** on alternate grid points, secure with masking tape and apply the paint (**f**).

Stencil C: Leaves

Repeat as for stencil **B**, filling in the gaps between the posy motif (**g**).

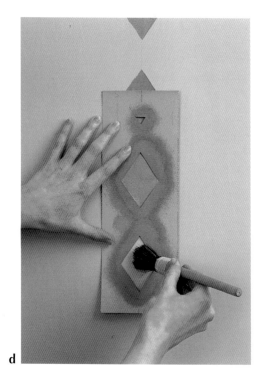

d

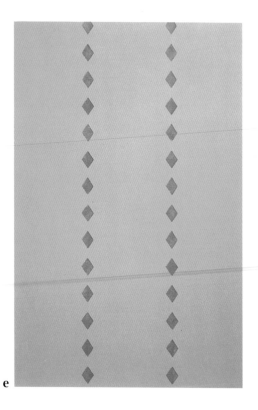

e

f

g

h

Second stencil color
Prepare the red milk paint following the method used for the first color.

Stencil D: Stripes and leaves
Position stencil **D** over the diamond design painted with stencil **A,** matching the diamond shapes as shown (**h**). Apply the red paint to create the stripes on the diamonds and the leaf motif (**i**).

Stencil E: Flowers and buds
Match the section of stem cut into stencil **E** with the design already painted with stencil **B,** and apply the red paint to form the flowers and buds of the posy (**j**). Do not paint the stem section with red, as this is used for positioning only.

i

j

Stenciling on wood

In the early nineteenth century, it was customary to paint the outsides of trunks and boxes, usually in dark green or black, or to give them a naive graining treatment. The insides were often lined with printed paper. This design, using widely available ready-mixed colors, is based on an American chest from the Shelburne Museum in Shelburne, Vermont (see p73). The original chest may have been decorated by a traveling painter when he was painting a room for a client. He would probably have employed the same colors and designs that were used on the walls.

A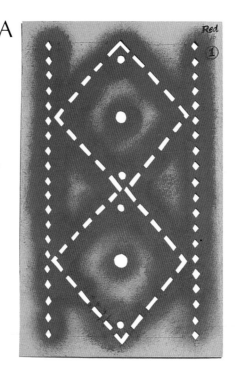

B

C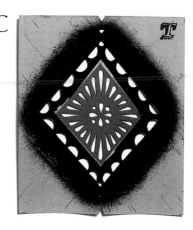

Scaling and cutting the stencils
On a three-dimensional object such as this wooden box, the stenciled pattern should be an exact fit on the most visible side. In this case, stencils **A** and **B** fit the box lid and the long sides of the box exactly six times lengthwise. Trace the stencils, scale them up to the appropriate size for your object, and using carbon paper transfer the design to stencil board. Cut out the stencils, including the four registration points on the left of stencil **B** and the two notches for registration on stencil **C**.

Base coat
Remove any handles and other hardware that would get in the way of the stenciling, and paint the box in the base color using the decorators' brush.

Stencil A: Border stage 1
Position stencil **A** against one edge of the box lid. Hold it in place with low-tack masking tape. Use a stencil brush to apply the first stencil color (**a**). Repeat along the other edge of the box lid.

Position the stencil against the edge of the front face of the box, aligning it so that it forms a continuation of the pattern on the lid. Paint as before, then repeat for the other edge of the front face and for the two edges of the back face (**b**).

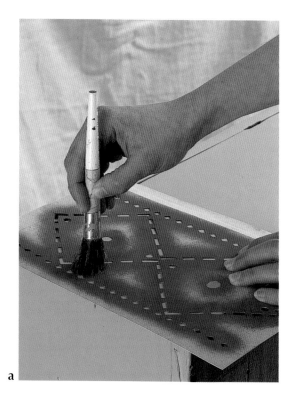
a

b

Stencil B: Border stage 2
Position the second stage of this border stencil over the pattern painted with stencil **A**, making sure the registration points align with the motif already stenciled. Hold the stencil in place with masking tape and apply the second stencil color (**c**). Repeat until all the borders are complete with the second color (**d**).

c

d

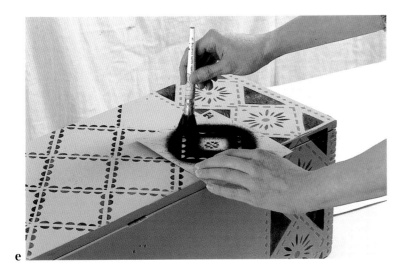

e

f

Stencil C: Stage 2
When the paint on stencil **C** is dry, remove the masking tape from the center and, using clear tape, mask off the edge. Position the stencil in the same positions as before, using the masked-off areas as registration points, and paint the centers of the pattern in red-brown milk paint (**g**).

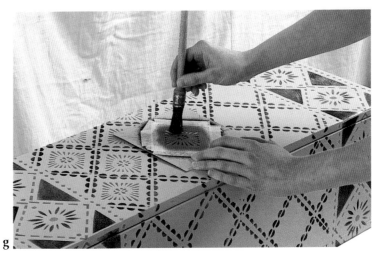

g

h

Stencil C: Stage 1
The pattern on the rest of the box is created by using the two paint colors with a single stencil. First, cover the central section of stencil **C** with masking tape. Position the stencil in the center of the box lid and apply black milk paint to the unmasked area (**e**). Repeat to cover the remainder of the box lid, working out from the center, then repeat again to cover the front and back faces and the ends of the box (**f**). The small triangle at the top of stencil **C** provides registration.

Finishing
When the stenciling is complete (**h**), replace the handles of the box and any other hardware. Apply a barrier coat of shellac varnish to protect the work, followed by a coat of wax polish. Use colored wax if you want an antique effect.

Freestyle details

Traditional designs for painted chairs of this kind used a small repertoire of motifs, popular because they were made up from a few simple brush strokes. The chair-painter of the early nineteenth century would not have drawn his design in place. He would have had a row of identical chairs to finish and would have known the pattern very well. Today's decorator should draw some guidelines in pencil.

Similar motifs can be traced, copied, or photocopied and enlarged to fit the space available. Once the design is the correct size for the chair being painted, transfer it to a piece of tracing paper. Mark the center of the design on the paper and match this to the center of the chair back. You may need to adjust the vertical positioning of the motif to achieve the best effect. Transfer the design to the chair back by drawing on the reverse of the tracing paper with soft pencil. Anchor the tracing paper with masking tape and lightly draw over the design in pencil.

The chair shown here has been given a gently distressed look by using a darker shade of green over a lighter base coat, but you could reverse the order of the coats to produce a slightly lighter effect.

OPPOSITE *A selection of alternative motifs for painted chairs.*

TOOLS AND EQUIPMENT

Base coat

Ready-mixed sage green milk paint diluted with water to the consistency of light cream

Top coat

Ready-mixed sage green milk paint mixed with a little red and diluted with water to the consistency of light cream

First freestyle color

Ready-mixed red-brown milk paint diluted with water to the consistency of light cream

Second freestyle color

Ready-mixed cream milk paint diluted with water to the consistency of light cream

1½in/40mm decorators' brush   Pencil
Long-bristled 1½in/40mm brush   Ruler
Soft brush   Fine lining brush
No. 8 artists' watercolor brush

Level of skill required Advanced
Recommended on Furniture, smooth walls

Base coats

Paint two coats of the base color to a solid finish using the 1½in/40mm brush (**a**).

Top coat

Brush the top coat on thinly and loosely using a long-bristled 1½in/40mm brush, to allow the base coat to show through (**b**). Use a soft, dry brush with a dabbing motion to stipple some of the top coat color around the turned areas of the chair. The top coat will look rather messy while wet, but will dry to give extra depth of color and a gently distressed effect.

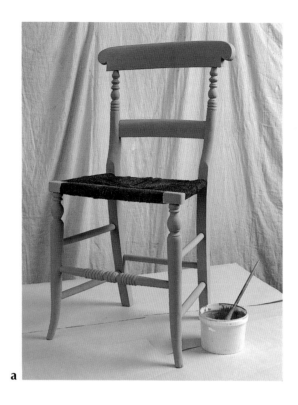

a

b

c

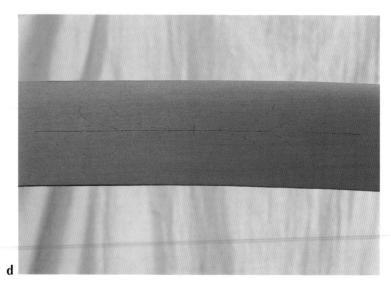

d

Painting the bottom rail and turnings

Using a No. 8 artists' watercolor brush, paint a line with the first freestyle color running across the center of the chair's bottom rail and around the chair's turnings (**c**).

Marking the guidelines on the top rail

Using a ruler, find the center of the chair's top rail. Lightly draw a 9½in/24cm horizontal line centered on this point (**d**). You can adjust the dimensions to suit the size of your chair.

Painting the top rail
Using the same brush and color again, paint over the pencil line. Paint the attached leaves and dots using simple, swift brushstrokes (**e**). Unevenly painted and spaced leaves will add to the naive charm of the finished chair.

e

Applying the second freestyle color
With a fine lining brush, use the second color to paint the highlights (**f**).

f

LATEX

Latex paint is one of the great success stories of the second half of the twentieth century. Before it became commercially available in the 1950s, soft and oil-bound distempers or flat oil paint were the only real options for painting walls. By the 1960s, however, latex paint had begun to take the market by storm.

Latex paint is a product of the petrochemical industry. Whereas the binder in distemper and milk paint is a natural product – size, or casein derived from skimmed milk – the binder or resin in latex is synthetic. It is produced from vinyl acetate (a monomer) which has been polymerized in water to create a suspension of tiny rubbery polyvinyl acetate (PVA) spheres, called a latex. Surfactants (soaps) stabilize the latex by forming a film at the surface of the spheres or droplets. Generally, two or more different vinyl or acrylic monomers are used together; these are known as copolymers. Acrylic polymers are generally more expensive than vinyl polymers, but they are hardwearing and have good resistance to sunlight. As the water evaporates from the paint, the tiny rubbery spheres become closely packed together and then fuse with each other to form a continuous thin film. As the particles coalesce, the pigment becomes embedded with them.

The many advantages of latex paints have led to their widespread use. They can be conveniently used straight from the can, although application is often improved if they are diluted a little. They are almost odor-free and quick drying, making them pleasant to handle and allowing a room to be used within hours of painting. They are available in any paint store and are sold in hundreds of different colors. Latex paints readily accept coloring by pure pigments, stainers, powder colors, gouache, and acrylics, so they can be easily adapted on site to the exact shade required. They are also available in a variety of different finishes from completely flat and matte to a slight soft sheen, not unlike eggshell paint. Flat latex has a higher proportion of coarse extender particles (china clay, silica, or chalk), creating a rougher surface that absorbs more dirt. However, all latex paints, but especially those with a slight sheen, can be washed clean without damage to the paint surface.

Latex paints adhere to most surfaces, even plasterboard and bare masonry. Application is simple. New plaster or plasterboard should be primed with diluted latex, shellac, or acrylic primer. Old latex cannot be satisfactorily sanded with sandpaper as the film tends to tear rather than abrade. Instead, simply over-paint – no base coat is required unless a dramatic color change is planned. Latex can even be used on factory-finished or oil-painted radiators, but ensure that the paint does not come into direct contact with iron or steel; otherwise, rust will result. A first coat of one of the vinyl acrylic latex primers designed for use on metal should prevent this.

One quart or two pints of latex used either undiluted or diluted just enough to make it brushable will cover approximately 17sq.ft/1.5sq.m. However, this will vary according to the paint manufacturer, the person applying the paint, the surface, the temperature of the room, and the materials. For a thin glaze or wash, the same wall might need about ½pt/250ml of paint extended with water and acrylic medium to make two pints.

Despite its great success, latex paint has certain drawbacks. One problem, especially relevant in the case of old or damp buildings, is that most latex paints dry as a completely impermeable film. This means that where latex is applied to damp surfaces or surfaces previously coated with breathable distemper or milk paint, the top coat of latex eventually peels off in unsightly strips as moisture trapped behind the paint works its way out.

One latex paint that is semipermeable, however, is contract latex, designed for application on recently plastered walls. It allows the plaster to complete its drying-out process without delaying decoration work. However, because it contains less binder and less of the opaque pigment titanium white (see p28), you may find that extra coats are needed to cover a surface completely.

Latex can be used for almost any decorative finish, although it can produce a rather characterless finished effect if it is applied flat. Because it dries fast – like all water-based paints – it can be used to achieve effects requiring several coats. Extended with water and acrylic medium, it can produce the thinnest veil of color or, when used in a comparatively strong mix, can create sponge prints (see pp108-9). In the combination of sponging and colorwashing, it can produce subtle distressed effects that evoke old plaster (pp104-7). Further decorative possibilities with latex include painting walls with stripes and checks (pp110-113), and simple *trompe l'oeil*, to create the impression of tiling (pp124-7).

The all-white room is a perennial, though demanding, favorite. Latex is the perfect paint to use for white walls because it is tough enough to be washed down regularly, and when it needs repainting, it dries quickly after each coat.

Latex is sold in a vast selection of ready-mixed colors, and although choosing the right one from a small sample card is difficult, the quick-drying time means color tests and adjustments can be made easily. Because of its excellent covering power, latex is a good paint to use if you want a solid, flat finish, as seen in the green bedroom (above). You can also create the type of broken-color effect seen in the dining room (opposite) by using a wash coat of deep brown flat latex diluted with water and acrylic medium over a base coat of crimson silk latex.

Simple colorwashing

In each of these recipes, the wash coat consists of two parts latex to one part acrylic medium, which is then diluted with water to the consistency of thin milk. The high proportion of acrylic medium increases the transparency of the wash coat without making it too watery and ensures that it will adhere to the surface. It is best to use a vinyl silk base coat when colorwashing, because the absorbent properties of flat latex reduce the effect of brushing on the wash coat. However, you can use a matte base if you are aiming for a subtle finish such as when the wash coat consists of a mix made from the base coat. Vinyl silk should only be used in the wash coat if a shiny finished surface is required. The examples shown opposite demonstrate the wide variety of color effects that can be achieved using ready-mixed latex and latex to which color has been added.

TOOLS AND EQUIPMENT

Matte or vinyl silk latex
Acrylic medium

Large decorators' brush
Coarse decorators' brush

Level of skill required
Simple
Recommended on
Smooth or uneven walls

Base coat
Use the large decorators' brush to apply the base coat to a solid finish, then let it dry completely.

Colorwashing
Use a coarse brush to apply the wash quickly with a loose crisscross motion, leaving definite brush marks (see also p46). Do not load the brush too heavily as this will cause the paint to drip. Be sure always to brush from dry paint into wet, as brushing from wet into dry can gouge holes in the wet paint.

Base coat
Rich blue flat latex

Wash coat
Base coat tinted with blue and black and diluted with water and acrylic medium

Base coat
Rich terracotta vinyl silk latex

Wash coat
Stone color flat latex diluted with
water and acrylic medium

Base coat
Stone color vinyl silk latex

Wash coat
Turquoise flat latex diluted
with water and acrylic medium

Base coat
Red vinyl silk latex

Wash coat
Deep brown flat latex diluted with
water and acrylic medium

The bold treatment on these high walls is held in check by the formal architectural framework. To achieve this effect, use a fairly bright, strong blue glazed over with a mix of a little of the same color, darkened with raw umber and diluted with acrylic medium. A finish like this wears well and will continue to look good for many years.

Colorwashing over sponging

By combining colorwashing and sponging, you can achieve a loose imitation of some of the textures and colors found in old plastered and colorwashed walls. Flat latex is versatile enough to provide both the opaque base coats and the transparent washes. You can mix your own base-coat color if you want, but because of the large quantity required, you may find it more convenient to buy ready-mixed paint. The washes or glazes are thinned with water, and acrylic medium is added for translucency and to ensure the washes adhere to the surface (see p130). Of the examples shown overleaf, the pink and yellow are simplest, having a base coat followed by a sponged coat and a single wash. The blue-green example has more depth with its base coat, sponged coat and two washes.

The surface can be smooth or uneven, although a textured surface would be difficult to work on and confusing to the eye. Subtlety is also essential for this technique – there should not be a great contrast between the colors used. In fact, in each of the examples here, at least one of the coats is mixed from one of the others. Extra richness of color and tone comes from deliberately leaving gaps in the sponged and washed coats of paint, so that other layers show through.

Base coat
Use a large decorators' brush to apply the base coat.

Sponged coat
Soak a damp sponge in the thinned sponging coat and thoroughly squeeze out excess paint. After testing on a board, dab lightly over the base coat, rotating the wrist clockwise and counterclockwise to avoid making too even a pattern (**a** and **b**). Aim to achieve a broken effect with some of the base coat still showing through.

a

b

TOOLS AND EQUIPMENT

Large decorators' brush
Natural sponge
Large glider
Board for testing colors and consistency

Flat latex
Acrylic medium

Level of skill required Intermediate
Recommended on Smooth or uneven walls

First wash

When the sponged coat is completely dry, use the decorators' brush to apply the first wash coat in a crisscross movement (**c** and **d**), testing for color and consistency on a board before tackling the wall. Let it dry.

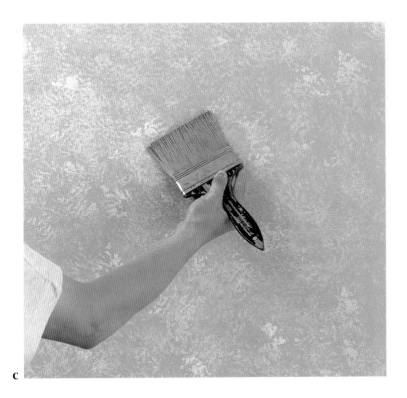

c

e

d

Second wash

Using the large decorators' brush again, apply the wash in the same crisscross movement as before, so that areas of the previous coats can be seen (**e**).

At its best, colorwashing over sponging resembles the effect of natural ageing rather than an applied technique. In this bedroom, broken and uneven colors and surfaces hold more interest than would plain colors. Using latex washes tinted with lemon yellow, yellow ocher and phthalo blue, as shown in the sample on the opposite page, would achieve a similarly restful effect.

Base coat
Stone flat latex

Base coat
Earth pink flat latex

Base coat
Light yellow ocher flat latex

Sponged coat
White flat latex

First wash
White flat latex tinted with lemon yellow,
yellow ocher, and phthalo blue

Sponged coat
Base coat tinted with Indian red

Sponged coat
Base coat mixed with white flat latex

Second wash
First wash mixed with white flat latex
and tinted with phthalo blue

Wash
Sponged coat mixed with white flat latex and
tinted with yellow ocher

Wash
Base coat tinted with cadmium yellow
and yellow ocher

Simple and layered sponging

Effects using one or more layers of sponging can easily be achieved using latex – this would not be possible with soft distemper (see p51) as further coats would "wake up" the base coat.

Although for colorwashing with latex a vinyl silk base coat is generally best, a flat-finish base coat is the most effective when sponging. This is because the paint is simply printed on the wall, rather than moved around the surface, and the slightly more absorbent base coat accepts the paint from the sponge more uniformly than a finish with a slight sheen would. Always test every coat on a piece of board before applying it to the final surface. The technique used for applying the paint is shown on page 100.

Base coat Green flat latex
Sponged coat Yellow flat latex

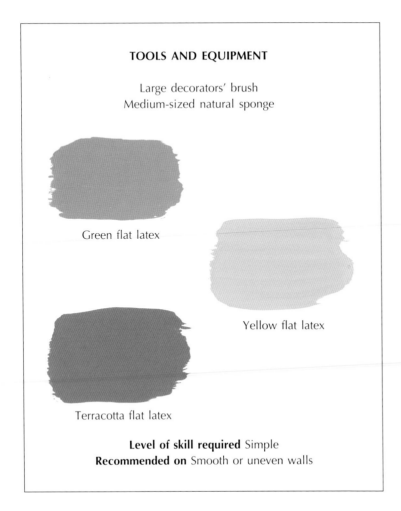

TOOLS AND EQUIPMENT

Large decorators' brush
Medium-sized natural sponge

Green flat latex

Yellow flat latex

Terracotta flat latex

Level of skill required Simple
Recommended on Smooth or uneven walls

Base coat Terracotta flat latex
First sponged coat Yellow flat latex
Second sponged coat Green flat latex

Base coat Terracotta flat latex
Sponged coat Green flat latex

Base coat Green flat latex
Sponged coat Terracotta flat latex

Base coat Green flat latex
First sponged coat Yellow flat latex
Second sponged coat Terracotta flat latex

Base coat Yellow flat latex
First sponged coat Green flat latex
Second sponged coat Terracotta flat latex

Sponging stripes

Using masking tape to create stripes – where the tape acts as a stencil – is rarely successful with a brushed finish. If the tape is not pressed down firmly enough, the paint bleeds underneath the edges, and if it is pressed down too hard, there is a real risk of pulling off the base coat. However, the use of a sponge means the tape does not need to be pressed down very firmly. Furthermore, the rough gritty texture of the sponging contrasts well with the mathematically straight edges of the masked stripes.

As with any sponged work, the edges can prove difficult to cover properly. Here, though, the strong and insistent pattern of the stripes will disguise much of this unevenness.

An elaboration of this technique would be to sponge a second coat of either the same color or a different color over the whole wall once the masking tape has been removed.

TOOLS AND EQUIPMENT

Base coat
White flat latex

Sponged color
White flat latex tinted with yellow ocher, burnt sienna, and lime yellow and diluted with water to the consistency of light cream

Large decorators' brush
Soft pencil
Ruler
Low-tack masking tape in ½in/12mm
and 1in/25mm widths
Medium-sized natural sponge

Level of skill required Simple
Recommended on Smooth walls

SPONGING STRIPES

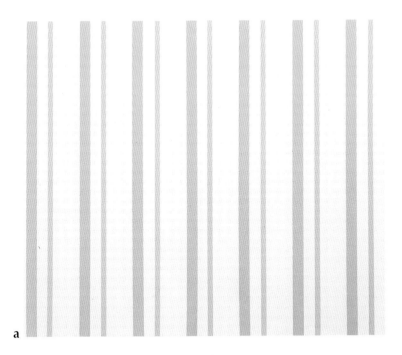

a

Base coat
Use the large decorators' brush to paint the base coat to a solid color, then let it dry completely.

Masking the wall
Mark the positions of the stripes along the top and bottom of the wall using a soft pencil and ruler. In this design, masking tape of ½in/12mm width alternates with tape of 1in/25mm width, with alternating gaps between them of 2½in/60mm and 1in/25mm. Apply masking tape to the wall at the marked positions (**a**).

Sponging the stripes
With a medium-sized natural sponge, apply the sponged color lightly all over the wall with a dabbing motion, rotating the wrist between prints (**b**). The technique is the same as for sponging with soft distemper (see p51). Remove the masking tape carefully while the paint is still wet to avoid lifting the latex from the wall (**c**). If left to dry, the latex could tear when the tape is removed.

b

c

Freestyle stripes and checks

Painting stripes or checks on a wall with latex is a remarkably simple and effective way of producing a distinctive wall decoration and of introducing colors drawn from curtains or upholstery. If the wall surface is smooth and even, with a bit of skill and patience you can create straight and true lines. However, freestyle stripes are rarely perfect, and uneven lines give a particular rustic effect which can be very appealing. It is more important to maintain the verticals and the spacing than to aim for absolutely straight edges. Paint the vertical stripes first; then, if you wish, you can add the horizontal lines to produce a check.

Using thinned-down paint for the stripes means that a convincing gingham effect is created where the lines cross and the two thicknesses of paint contrast with the single one elsewhere.

TOOLS AND EQUIPMENT

Base coat
String-colored flat latex

Stripe color
Cream flat latex diluted with water to the
consistency of light cream

Large decorators' brush
Chalk
Plumb line
Ruler
1½in/40mm glider

Level of skill required Intermediate
Recommended on Smooth walls

a

b

Base coat

Using a large decorators' brush, paint the base coat to a solid color and let it dry completely.

Painting the stripes

Mark vertical lines on the wall at 3in/80mm intervals using a ruler, plumb line, and chalk.

Standing completely square to the wall, paint the stripes using a 1½in/40mm glider, using the chalk lines as a guide for the center of the stripes (**a**). A glider holds a lot of paint, making it possible to achieve fairly long strokes with one brush load. Work from the top of the wall to the bottom, applying even pressure on the brush. As lines between brushstrokes are inevitable, try to make sure that the lines appear at different places in adjacent rows. Step back from the work from time to time to check that the stripes are even. Repeat until all the stripes are complete (**b**), then leave to dry.

Painting the checks

Using the 1½in/40mm glider filled with the stripe color, paint the horizontal stripes (**c**). The positions of these may be marked with chalk and a ruler at 3in/80mm intervals, or they can be judged by eye, matching line spacing and thickness to produce the squares.

c

Distressing wood

This technique, which mimics the effect of old paintwork, works best on coarse-grained rough wood with well-defined knots. Pine is ideal, and it can be enhanced still further by scraping with a wire brush along the grain. It is not possible to achieve the same effect with close-grained woods such as mahogany and beech.

Distressing wooden furniture to mimic the look achieved by natural aging involves a lot of hard work, but the end product is well worth the effort. On a naturally distressed piece, the paintwork would become more worn around the knots, around edges and corners, and at floor level, where it would have been kicked and scuffed over the years. Using sandpaper, you can carefully control the amount of paint removed, working harder at these areas to create an authentic finished effect.

TOOLS AND EQUIPMENT

Bright blue flat latex

Wire brush   Coarse sandpaper
3in/80mm decorators' brush   Wood block

Level of skill required Simple
Recommended on Woods with a pronounced grain

Painting the wood
Vigorously scrape the wood with a wire brush along the grain to expose its natural pattern. Steel wool is not suitable here as it would leave black stains on the light wood. Use the decorators' brush to apply two coats of flat latex, brushing the paint well into all the hollows and depressions (**a**). Leave to dry completely.

Distressing
With coarse sandpaper wrapped around a block of wood, rub the paint down vigorously in the direction of the grain until the desired effect is achieved (**b** and **c**). Work the sandpaper well around any knots to reveal the pattern of the grain.

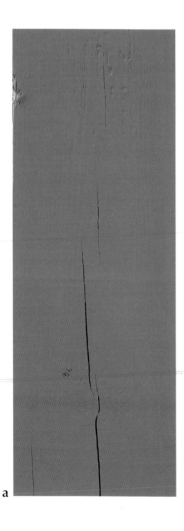

a

b

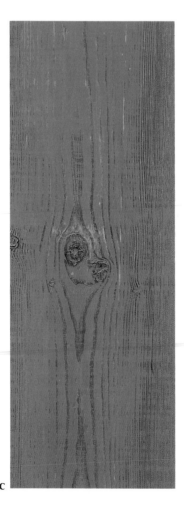

c

114

The inspiration for this project is an old cupboard from Santa Fe, New Mexico – home to an artists' colony in the 1920s – which has stood the test of time despite heavy wear and tear.

Pickled wood

Creating a pickled effect on wood first became fashionable during the late nineteenth century under the influence of the Arts and Crafts movement. The look harked back to the sixteenth and seventeenth centuries, when limewash or whitewash was applied for protection to woodwork as well as to plastered walls. Here we show how it is possible to create a pickled effect without resorting to buying one of the special commercially produced pickling preparations.

Pickling should be carried out on an open-grained wood such as oak or ash, which should not be varnished or polished. If a strong contrast between the wood and the pickling is desired, the wood can be darkened with a water-based wood stain. In the case of oak, as shown here, ammonia is traditionally used for a dark stain.

TOOLS AND EQUIPMENT

Flat white latex
Old 2in/50mm brush
Lint-free rag or
Paper towels
Medium steel wool

Level of skill required Simple
Recommended on
Dark wood with a coarse grain

a

b

c

Using a worn 2in/50mm brush, work the latex deep into the grain of the wood, then rub it off the surface almost immediately with a lint-free rag or paper towel (**a**). Make sure you work the paint well into any quirks or moldings in the wood. This whole operation needs to be carried out quickly as the paint dries fast, so only work on a small area at a time.

When the paint is dry, emphasize any quirks or moldings by lightly rubbing them over with medium steel wool (**b** and **c**).

OPPOSITE *Understated pickling imparts character by creating the impression of years of use. This elaborate pickled oak settle contrasts well with the bright white walls and floor.*

Painted stenciling

This design is based on a pattern decorating a passage in the servants' quarters of a large, early nineteenth-century house, in which a Greek key pattern is stencilled at dado level. The original wall design was applied in oil-based paint below the dado and in distemper above. This is because the wall below the dado needed to be given a more durable finish to protect it against the backs of chairs that were placed there. Latex is a perfectly appropriate modern alternative, although if you are using the pattern at dado level, it would be practical to paint below the dado with vinyl silk latex because it gives a more durable, easy-to-clean finish for an area that receives most wear and tear. Painting the baseboard the same color as the stencil pattern would add an effective finishing touch.

A correctly proportioned dado line should be about 30in/75cm from the floor. A repeating stencil design such as this could also be used for a frieze or a door frame, or in any place where a decorative border would add elegance.

TOOLS AND EQUIPMENT

Base coat
Yellowish-cream flat latex

Second color
Ox-blood vinyl silk latex

Stencil color
Second color tinted with black

Stencil
Large decorators' brush
Soft pencil
Chalk line (optional)
Straightedge
Masking tape (optional)
Carpenter's level
Old knife or small brush
Palette, old plate, or jar lid
Stencil brush

Level of skill required
Intermediate
Recommended on
Smooth walls

Cutting the stencil
Trace, scale up, and cut out the stencil as shown on page 83. Here a section of the continuing pattern has been cut out and covered with clear tape to provide registration points.

Base coat
Using a large decorators' brush, paint the entire wall with the base coat to a solid finish and let it dry completely.

Second coat
Draw a light pencil line or snap a chalk line across the wall at dado height. Paint the second color to a solid finish below the dado line and let it dry completely (**a**). You may find it useful to paint parallel to a straightedge placed along the line, or to use masking tape to achieve a clean line (but see page 110).

a

b

Painting the stencil

With an old knife or small brush, dab a little of the stencil color onto a palette, old plate, or jar lid. Charge the stencil brush with the paint by working it well into the bristles, ensuring that the brush is not overloaded with paint. Starting at the right-hand side of the wall, position the bottom of the stencil on the dado line and apply the paint using a dabbing or brushing motion (see p84). Move the stencil to the left until the registration points line up with the painted pattern, and stencil again (**b**). Repeat along the wall until the design is complete.

Stenciling using a sponge

A piece of eighteenth-century damask was the inspiration for this project. The two-tone coloring and slight sheen is typical of the appearance of this material, and the cross-dragged background imitates the warp and weft of woven silk or linen. Sponging through the stencil gives a different effect from that produced by a brush and cleverly contrasts with the cross-dragged background to give the impression of a woven pattern.

The stencil was designed with a finial at the top of alternate bands of stenciling. It is used only at the top of the wall and does not appear elsewhere in the design. The two curved lines at the bottom of the stencil provide registration points.

TOOLS AND EQUIPMENT

Base coat
Bright yellow-green vinyl silk latex

Glaze coats
Base coat tinted with blue, yellow ocher, and yellow, mixed with six to seven times its own volume of acrylic scumble, then thinned with water to the consistency of light cream

Stencil color
Base coat tinted with blue, yellow ocher, black, and a little burnt umber, then diluted with water to the consistency of heavy cream

Large decorators' brush
Coarse-bristled 4in/10cm brush
Stencil
Plumb line and straightedge
Chalk
Masking tape
Palette, old plate, or jar lid
Medium-sized natural sponge

Level of skill required Advanced
Recommended on Smooth walls

a

Base coat
Use the large decorators' brush to apply the base coat to a solid color, then let it dry completely.

Applying the glaze
When the base coat is dry, apply a coat of glaze and drag or "lay off" with continuous vertical strokes using a coarse-bristled 4in/ 10cm brush (**a**). The base coat should show through the dragged glaze coat. Let it dry for at least twelve hours.

Use the same brush to drag a second coat of glaze horizontally across the first (**b** and **c**) and let it dry for at least twelve hours.

Cutting the stencil
Trace, scale up, and cut out the stencil as described on page 83.

Marking the stencil lines
Using a plumb line and straightedge, mark the wall with vertical chalk lines spaced to correspond with the center line of the pattern. Holding the stencil up to the wall, mark where the top of the lower columns of stencils should start in order to interlock neatly with the columns topped by finials, and mark this horizontal line with chalk.

b

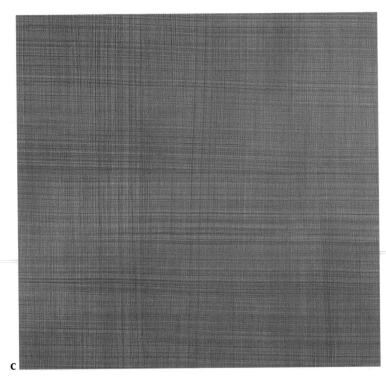

c

Painting the stencil

Transfer a small quantity of stencil color to a palette, old plate, or jar lid. Wet a medium-sized natural sponge with water; squeeze it out completely, then dip it into the paint. Work it into the sponge so that it is not overloaded. Apply the paint through the stencil with a dabbing motion (**d**).

Stencil the columns topped with the finials first, lining up the center of the stencil with alternate vertical lines and holding the stencil in place with masking tape. Let it dry and mask out the finial design. When stenciling the lines without finials, align the top of the first stencil with the chalk line drawn for this purpose, to ensure a uniform pattern.

Do not worry about applying the paint too evenly as it is part of the intended effect of this type of design that some parts should appear denser than others.

123

Trompe l'oeil tiles

This design is inspired by an eighteenth-century Delft tile. Because such tiles were produced in their thousands, they were painted very quickly and roughly with resulting variations from tile to tile. When copying the design, it is more important to use swift confident brushstrokes, producing an effect similar in spirit to the original, than to slavishly imitate a design.

You can copy the central motif of the tiles from various sources to suit the look of your room, or they can be omitted altogether. This design is ideal for kitchens or bathroom areas or around a fireplace, but, where the paint will be subject to heavy wear, a coat of gloss acrylic varnish will protect the paintwork and allow for regular wiping down.

In seventeenth-century Holland, a baseboard of Delft tiles was commonly set flush with the wall. This would protect the distempered wall surface from the constant mopping and washing of the tiled or marble floor. It is possible to create this look with the trompe l'oeil effect shown here, provided the baseboard is protected with a coat of acrylic varnish.

The dark white of the base coat has been carefully matched to the original Delft tile, though it might seem surprisingly far from the white color one would expect.

TOOLS AND EQUIPMENT

Base coat
White flat latex tinted with black, yellow ocher, blue, and burnt umber, and diluted with water to the consistency of light cream

Joint line color
Dark gray flat latex

Delft blue
White flat latex tinted with blue, black, and burnt umber

Decorators' brush
Soft pencil
Straightedge
Carpenter's level
Fine lining brush
Palette, old plate, or jar lid
Board for testing technique

Level of skill required
Advanced
Recommended on Small areas, smooth surfaces

a

b

Preparing and marking the wall
Use the decorators' brush to apply two coats of base color to a solid finish and let it dry completely. With a soft pencil, straightedge, and level, divide the area to be painted into 5in/12cm squares – the size of the original tile reproduced on p125 (**a**).

Painting the joint lines
With a fine lining brush, apply the joint line color along the pencil lines to create the effect of joint lines (**b**). Work freestyle and from time to time apply a little extra pressure to the brush, thickening the line in places to reproduce the irregular appearance of the original joint lines.

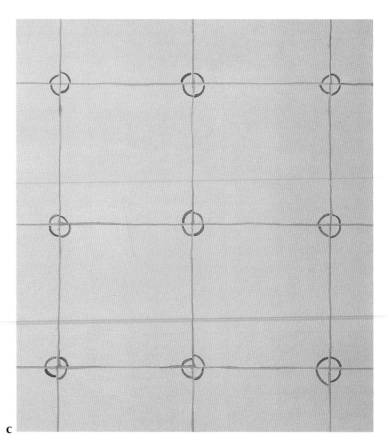

Painting the corner motifs
Place a small amount of the Delft blue color on a palette, old plate, or jar lid. Fill the lining brush with the paint, which should be diluted slightly with water as work proceeds. Paint the quarter circles in the four corners of each tile before moving onto the next. The circle at the corner where the four painted tiles meet should be irregular, as it would be if real tiles were used (**c**). Make sure the blue does not cross the joint lines that separate the tiles. **c**

d

e

Completing the design
Copy the decorative flourishes of the corner design on the original tile shown on p125 (**d**). It is best to set up a rhythm of work by painting just one part of each motif in turn, then moving on to the same part on the next corner, rather than tackling a whole corner at once.

Complete the wall by painting an occasional central motif as shown (**e** and **f**), based on these or other suitable designs on Delft tiles. Because the motifs are painted entirely freestyle without pencil guidelines, practice on a board until you are confident.

f

Acryli
'artists'

cs and

paints

The most exciting and innovative ideas being developed in paint today involve the use of acrylics. Acrylic resins were first formulated in Germany in 1901 by Otto Röhm, and produced commercially in the United States of America from the 1930s by the firms of Röhm & Haas and by E.I. DuPont de Nemours. These early resins were tried out in a variety of articles, from false teeth through household utensils to aircraft windows.

Acrylic polymers derived from resins quickly proved useful in paint manufacture because their qualities provide a perfect binder for pigments. Traditional binders – linseed oil, egg, gum, wax, milk, beer, and size – are all natural and domestic products which have been adapted for use in paint. However, they all have certain disadvantages. For example, an emulsion of egg and water can only accommodate a certain quantity of pigment and does not adhere well to all surfaces. Such limitations do not apply to acrylic polymers.

When acrylic resins are converted into emulsions (polymerized) in water, they become milky white, but as the water evaporates and the emulsions dry, they leave a crystal-clear film. This film has the advantages of being tough and flexible, insoluble in water, rotproof and resistant to discoloration and cracking.

Paints made with acrylic polymers – known as acrylic or polymer colors – have a depth and brilliance of color unmatched by other types of paint. The pigments that can be used are virtually the same as those employed to color other types of paint, except that the only white is titanium dioxide. Acrylic paints adhere to almost any surface, and can be thinned and easily washed out of brushes with water. They dry to form a tough, flexible film impervious to water.

Because of their versatility, acrylic paints have been popular with artists since they were introduced in the 1950s. At around the same time, solvent-borne acrylics were developed as car paints, but since the late 1980s these have been superseded by the more environmentally acceptable water-borne acrylics. Acrylic paints are now being developed for use in home decoration; as such they are a welcome, hard-wearing, and weather-resistant addition to the available range of water-soluble paints. Public feeling, the decorating trade, and the manufacturing industry are all contributing to a growing interest in and demand for acrylic paints, which seem destined to oust solvent-based paints for most applications.

Available in gloss or flat finishes, acrylic paints can be bought for internal or external use, as primer, top coat, varnish, floor coating, and wood stain. They are also available as masonry paint in smooth or textured finishes. Some manufacturers have even developed acrylic rust-free paint systems for use on metals (see pp134-5). When used for large areas of plain painting, acrylic paint suffers from the same disadvantage as latex paint, namely a rather mechanical, uniform appearance. This can, however, be counteracted by varnishing with flat acrylic medium (see below), which gives an attractive, non-reflective surface.

Acrylic paint for home decoration tends to come in strong bright colors, but it is possible to mix any color by using stainers. A much wider choice of colors is available in the artists' color lines, and these can be bought in tubes as a thickish paste, or in jars or bottles if a more fluid consistency is required. Naturally, with their higher concentration of pigment, artists' colors are more expensive than decorators' paint. As a result, artists' acrylics are more commonly used for small projects such as marbling a picture mat (see pp152-3) or for creating a decorative finish on a small object (pp156-9).

Acrylic polymers also form the basis of another selection of acrylic products that are immensely useful for today's decorating techniques. Acrylic varnishes in gloss or flat finishes can serve as a protective, non-yellowing coat, and can also be tinted to create translucent effects. Acrylic medium, also available in gloss or flat-finish, has several uses. Indeed the subtler, broken-color effects of acrylic paint rely on the addition of some acrylic medium. At its simplest, acrylic medium can be used as a varnish or to strengthen a paint, particularly soft distemper, to which it will impart a slightly more robust surface. When diluting latex paint with water to make a wash, the addition of some acrylic medium will help to make the latex translucent and ensure that the resulting wash is not too weak. For a very translucent but strong wash, use just acrylic medium with water and a small quantity of pigment.

Acrylic scumble is the water-based, non-yellowing equivalent of oil scumble, a colorless glaze for broken-color work. Formulated to hold brush marks when stippling and combing (see pp142-3) and graining (pp144-9), scumble may be thinned with water, but if it is

The water-resistant quality of acrylics makes them ideal for use in bathrooms, where they will stand up well to splashes. They are suited to plain painting and are sold in a choice of clear, bright colors such as those seen in this Moorish-style bathroom. Here, a border and decorative embellishments in shocking pink are set against a background of mint green. The walls are given an extra dimension by the colored light shed by the Moroccan lantern and wall fittings.

over-thinned, it ceases to hold the brush strokes and instead starts to foam. This in itself produces a curious decorative effect that can be useful in marbling and certain sorts of antiquing, and for simulating patinated bronze.

In general, it is best to buy the most expensive acrylic products you can afford. They will contain better pigments and the latest refinements in quality as manufacturers constantly improve the paints – an important factor in this relatively new field. It is also advisable to work with only one product line. This reduces the risk of one manufacturer's formulation containing ingredients that might react badly with another's.

Another type of artists' paint that is useful for the home decorator – especially for smaller projects – is gouache. Also known as poster paint or body color, gouache is an opaque watercolor paint bound with size, casein, or acrylic. The usual artists' gouache is the rewettable kind bound with size – the casein and acrylic-bound varieties are water resistant when dry.

Although none of the techniques described in this book rely on gouache alone, with the addition of beer, it can be used to create a graining effect (see pp144-7). It can also be employed as a coloring agent in much the same way as artists' acrylics, being a useful source of strong pure pigment. Like acrylics, gouache is available in tubes from artists' suppliers.

LEFT *Acrylics are a good choice for painting outdoor furniture, because their toughness makes them hard wearing and weather resistant. It is a good idea to add a top coat of acrylic varnish for extra protection on chairs or tables that are left outside. Here, green stripes relieve the uniform appearance of the blue chairs.*

RIGHT *The ease with which a tube of artists' acrylic paint can be squeezed onto a palette and diluted with enough water to make it brushable means that it is an excellent medium to use for freestyle painting. This lighthearted pattern of fish and scrolls is a happy complement to the marble corner sink and the shelf.*

Painting iron

This project uses an acrylic paint system specially designed for ferrous metal. Before the development of this system, rusty metal objects had to be stripped with chemical strippers, mechanically cleaned and primed with rust-inhibiting primer, and then finished with a traditional oil-based paint. An acrylic-based system, by contrast, not only obviates the need for these products and processes, but also offers extra benefits in that brushes can be washed out in water (if cleaned promptly after use), the work is completed very quickly, and the resulting coat is comparatively thin, so is unlikely to clog decorative detail. This system gives you the choice of two primers: a low-build one for ordinary use, and a high-build version for use where there is a large amount of rust. Similar acrylic paint systems are available for galvanized metal and aluminum.

TOOLS AND EQUIPMENT

Acrylic anticorrosive primer
Quick-drying acrylic mid-coat paint
for ferrous metal
Acrylic finish coat for ferrous metal

Wire brush
Small brush

Level of skill required Simple
Recommended on Metal

Preparing the surface

Remove all loose rust and paint with a wire brush (**a**). The surface should appear dark brown with occasional bright metallic streaks.

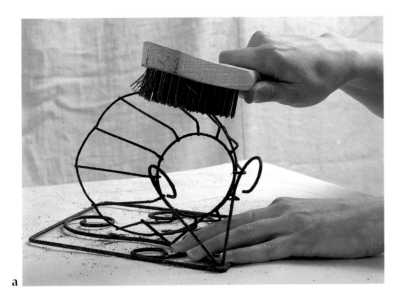

a

Primer

Thoroughly stir the anticorrosive primer and apply two coats with a small brush (**b**). The primer turns clear with a slight satin sheen within a few minutes, leaving the browns of any rust highlighted. You can apply the second coat of primer after half an hour, but let it dry for two and a half hours before applying the mid-coat.

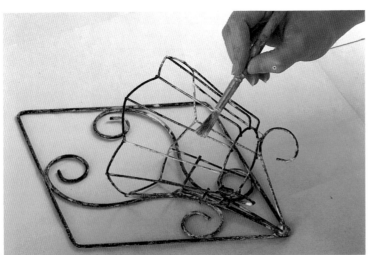

b

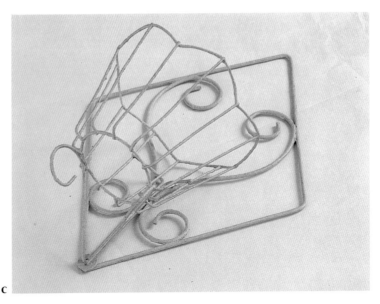

c

Mid-coat

Stir the quick-drying acrylic mid-coat thoroughly and apply (**c**). Let it dry completely.

d

Finish coat

When the mid-coat is completely dry – allow four hours before recoating – apply one or more coats of the finish (**d**).

Verdigris

Verdigris is the name given to the patina that develops when bronze, copper, or brass is exposed to the elements over a long period of time. Acrylic-based glazes are particularly suitable for creating a verdigris finish. Subtle layers of glaze can be built up and, because the glazes are quick drying, they can be applied in varying thicknesses to mimic the color and texture of real verdigris. This project uses two glaze coats, but it is worth experimenting with additional glazes. You could, for example, add a third, almost white glaze applied very sparingly. This paint effect is best used on objects that could realistically be made from metal – candlesticks, furniture legs, boxes, vases, or sculpture.

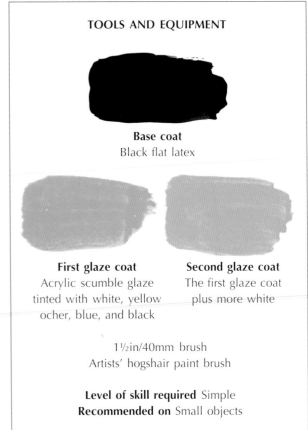

TOOLS AND EQUIPMENT

Base coat
Black flat latex

First glaze coat
Acrylic scumble glaze tinted with white, yellow ocher, blue, and black

Second glaze coat
The first glaze coat plus more white

1½in/40mm brush
Artists' hogshair paint brush

Level of skill required Simple
Recommended on Small objects

Base coat
Paint the candlestick in the base coat to a solid color using the 1½in/40mm brush. Let it dry completely.

Stippling the first glaze coat
With the stiff bristles of the hogshair paint brush lightly filled with paint, stipple on the first glaze coat (**a**). Try to avoid too even a finish. Let it dry completely (**b**).

a

b

Stippling the second glaze coat
Apply the second glaze coat in the same way as the first, but less evenly (**c**). Apply this second coat very lightly around the turnings, so that the hollows are left darker.

The finished candlestick (**d**) should be left unvarnished to conserve the rough texture created by the stippling.

c

d

Bronzed finish and gold leaf

Bronze comes in many different colors. Bright from the foundry, it looks like brass, but when treated with different chemicals or lacquers, it can be greenish, brownish, reddish, and even black. Here a medium-brown color has been achieved using a number of semitranslucent glazes. Leaving the prominent parts of an object paler gives the appearance of wear.

The decorative gilding has been applied using transfer gold leaf and acrylic gold size. The gold leaf is generally sold by art suppliers in 3½in/85mm squares. When rubbed, the gold will transfer from its backing paper to the size, which acts as an adhesive. This kind of gilding was previously done with oil-based size, and it is only recently that an acrylic size, or mordant, has been developed. Here, the technique is used to transform a plain wooden candlestick.

TOOLS AND EQUIPMENT

Base coat
Bright mustard yellow
flat latex

Glaze coat
Acrylic medium tinted with yellow
ocher, black, blue, and raw umber,
and diluted with water to the
consistency of light cream

Finish coat
Satin finish acrylic varnish

1½in/40mm brush
1½in/40mm glider
Medium lining brush
Acrylic gold size
3-4 sheets of transfer gold leaf
Stiff small brush cut down to ½in/12mm or cotton pad
Dusting brush, badger softener, or cotton balls

Level of skill required Intermediate
Recommended on Small objects such as boxes or candlesticks

Base coat
Use the 1½in/40mm brush to paint the candlestick to a solid color using the base coat color. Let it dry completely.

Glaze coats
Use the 1½in/40mm glider to apply three or four coats of the glaze (**a**). Brush on smoothly. After the final coat, the yellow base coat should be just visible through the glaze, except where the glaze coat has been allowed to build up in the hollows of the candlestick.

Applying the size
Using a medium lining brush, apply acrylic gold size to the bands to be gilded (**b**).

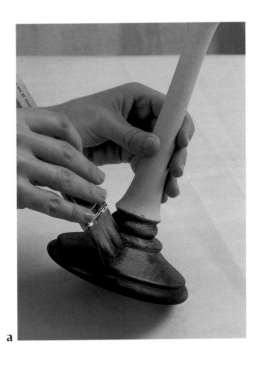

a

b

c

d

Gilding
When the size is dry but still slightly tacky, use your finger, the small cut-down brush, or a cotton pad to rub the gold transfer leaf down onto the sized areas (**c**). Work on a small area at a time. The gold leaf will only adhere to the size, leaving a layer of bright gilding.

Leave overnight to dry, then use a dusting brush, badger softener, or cotton ball to brush off the excess gold.

Finishing
Apply a coat of satin finish acrylic varnish to the bronzed areas (**d**).

Colorwashing and antiquing

In the first half of this century, before stripped pine became so popular in the 1960s and 1970s, almost all wood was painted. Kitchen cabinets and hutches would have had scrubbed wooden tops and painted shelves and doors. With use, the paint would develop an attractive patina of wear. It is possible to simulate the results of this aging process using simple paint techniques on new or previously painted wood. Any degree of simulated age can be achieved. The end result should be a soft, mellow look.

White acrylic primer, tinted to the appropriate color, is used as the base coat because it is inexpensive, readily available, and hardwearing.

TOOLS AND EQUIPMENT

Priming coat
White acrylic primer

Base coat
White acrylic primer tinted with yellow ocher, lime yellow, black, blue, and raw umber, then diluted with water to the consistency of heavy cream

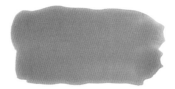

Wash coat glaze
Acrylic medium tinted with blue, yellow ocher, raw umber, and black, then diluted to a watery consistency

Antiquing glaze
Acrylic medium tinted with raw umber and a very small amount of black, then diluted to a watery consistency

2in/50mm brush
1½in/40mm glider
Lint-free cloth

Level of skill required Intermediate
Recommended on Wooden furniture

Primer and base coat

Using the 2in/50mm brush, paint the cupboard with acrylic primer. Then, using the same brush, apply the base coat to a solid color. Let it dry completely.

Wash coat glaze

When the base coat is dry, use a 1½in/40mm glider to brush on the wash coat glaze loosely, following the grain of the wood (**a**). The fine bristles of the glider create an attractive imprint in the wash coat glaze. Let it dry completely (**b**).

a

b

Antiquing glaze

To simulate greater age, brush on the antiquing glaze with the glider (**c**). Before this coat dries, wipe off some glaze from the center of the door panel with a piece of lint-free cloth. The resulting unevenness should produce a more authentic look (**d**). The antique effect can be enhanced by applying more than one coat of glaze in places.

c

d

Stippling and combing

The combination of stippling, combing, and brush-dragging can produce different tones of the same color. Stippling, in removing the glaze, makes a very pale and even texture. Combing looks coarser and leaves more areas of solid color. Combing twice, with slightly different rhythms, would produce a moiré effect; cross-combing a check.

The finished effect can be as quiet or strident as you want. On the whole it would be best to use these finishes on their own to unify a variety of cupboard doors and drawer fronts rather than to muddle an already complicated scheme involving other paint effects. If the surface to be painted is laminated, it should be roughened with medium sandpaper to provide a key and primed with acrylic primer.

TOOLS AND EQUIPMENT

Base coat
Turquoise vinyl silk latex

Glaze coat
Slow-set acrylic scumble glaze tinted with blue and black, then diluted with water to the consistency of light cream

2in/50mm brush
Rubber stippler
Lining fitch
Fine graining comb
Gloss acrylic varnish (optional)

Level of skill required Intermediate
Recommended on Paneled wooden furniture

Base coat
Using a 2in/50mm brush, apply the base coat to a solid finish. Let it dry completely.

Applying the glaze coat to the panels
Use the same brush to apply the glaze coat to the cupboard door panels and moldings, but not the rails and stiles (**a**).

a

b

Stippling the panels
While the glaze is still wet, stipple the panels with a rubber stippler (**b**). Use a fast but gentle dabbing motion, keeping the stippler moving and turning continuously to break up the glaze.

c

Finishing the edges
Draw a lining fitch through the glaze on the moldings to make the edges neat (**c**).

Graining the stiles and rails
Using the 2in/50mm brush, apply glaze to the stiles and rails and to the outside edges of the cupboard door (**d**). Lay off the glaze smoothly in the direction of the grain, following the guidelines for painting stiles and rails (see p34).

Combing
While the glaze coat is still wet, lightly pull a fine graining comb through the glaze in the direction of the grain (**e**). A tremulous motion of the hand will achieve a wavy effect. Comb the top and bottom rails of the door first, then re-brush the ends of the stiles before combing them. Let it dry completely (**f**).

Finishing
In areas subject to heavy wear, apply a coat of gloss acrylic varnish.

d

e

f

Oak graining

Graining can be used nowadays, as in the eighteenth and nineteenth centuries, to make cheap softwood look like a more expensive hardwood. Traditionally, pigment alone was used with stale beer to create the graining glaze. However, decorators these days find it more convenient to use gouache, which is an excellent source of rich, pure color. The added binder present in gouache strengthens the glaze, although it still remains soft enough to wipe away where necessary. The stickiness of the beer holds the glaze, keeping it workable. Using water would produce a much thinner glaze which would not be so easy to handle.

The base coat needs to stay sound when the graining is added, so this technique works best carried out on a vinyl silk latex base coat. Flat latex can be used, but it should be followed with a coat of acrylic glaze to stop it from absorbing the graining coat too fast. Before starting to grain, study the character of the wood to be emulated, just as when marbling.

TOOLS AND EQUIPMENT

Base coat
White vinyl silk latex tinted with raw umber, yellow ocher, and burnt umber

Graining glaze
Raw umber and yellow ocher gouache diluted with flat beer to the consistency of light cream

Large decorators' brush
2in/50mm brush
Comb or graining brush
Lint-free cloth
Dusting brush or badger softener
White shellac
Acrylic varnish

Level of skill required Intermediate
Recommended on Woodwork, furniture

Base coat
Use the large decorators' brush to apply the base coat to create a solid and smooth finish, because any brush marks will show through the graining. For this and the remaining coats, work in the order of painting doors recommended on page 34. Let it dry completely.

a

b

c

Applying the graining glaze

Use the 2in/50mm brush to apply the glaze evenly, ensuring that the base coat is adequately covered.

Using most of the length of the bristles and working in the direction of the grain, draw the brush through the wet graining glaze with a sweeping, slightly trembling motion (**a**). The impression of the bristles should be left in the glaze. If the glaze flows out and loses definition, wipe it off, add more gouache, and reapply.

Combing and softening the glaze

Use a comb or graining brush to break up the lines of the brush marks (**b**). Draw the comb lightly through the glaze – too much pressure will scratch the base coat. The comb should cross the brush lines at a gentle angle, breaking the lines into long thin blade shapes. If the comb does not succeed in breaking up the brush lines, wipe off the glaze with a lint-free cloth, add a little more beer to the mix, and reapply. If the effect is too harsh, use a dry dusting brush or a badger softener to soften the lines in the glaze before it dries (**c**).

Varnishing

Brush on two coats of white shellac followed by one or two coats of acrylic varnish to protect the surface (**d**). The shellac seals the glaze, preventing it from being "picked up" when the acrylic varnish is applied.

d

Mahogany graining

In the eighteenth century, mahogany graining would have been considered a cut above the oak or wainscot graining seen on pp144-5. At that time, mahogany was extensively used for doors, but the real thing was expensive even then, and often a substitute would be used, either chocolate-colored paint – plain and unfigured – or the glazed graining shown here.

It takes a lot of practice to master some of the flowery patterns of "feathered" mahogany, but a simple "straight-grained" simulation is not difficult and can be very effective. Simple, inexpensive modern cupboards – plain or paneled – can be lifted and given color and interest with a simple brush-grained finish. The color of natural mahogany is very variable, so this effect could be carried out in any color from blackish red to a pale gingery brown.

TOOLS AND EQUIPMENT

Base coat
Pinkish-red vinyl silk latex

Graining glaze
Burnt umber gouache and black water stainer diluted with flat beer to the consistency of light cream

Large decorators' brush
2in/50mm brush
Badger softener
White shellac
Acrylic varnish

Level of skill required Intermediate
Recommended on Woodwork, furniture

Base coat
Using the large decorators' brush, apply the base coat to create a solid and smooth finish. For this and the graining coats, follow the order of painting doors recommended on page 34. Let it dry completely.

Applying the graining glaze
Using the 2in/50mm brush, apply the glaze coat in every direction, working on one element at a time, and immediately lay off in the direction of the grain (**a**). Vary the amount of glaze on the brush to ensure that some bands of glaze are darker than others.

Softening
With a dry badger softener, soften the finish slightly by barely skimming the surface of the glaze across the grain and moving in one direction only (**b**).

Flogging
Using the side of the badger softener, tap the length of the bristles gently against the glaze (known as flogging) (**c**). Always move the brush forward or upward, working over the marks left by the previous strokes. Flogging the surface lightly produces an effect which imitates the pores in real mahogany.

Varnishing
Finish with two coats of white shellac followed by one or two coats of acrylic varnish to protect the surface (**d**).

Rosewood graining

The unusual swirling grain of rosewood was much favored throughout the last century for its decorative qualities. Usually employed as a veneer, rarely as solid wood because of its cost, the wood derives from several different trees native to India and South America, the South American variety being that most commonly used in North America.

The name comes both from the color and from the scent the wood gives off when it is cut. The look of rosewood was often imitated, sometimes, as here, in paint, and sometimes by staining a plainer wood, usually beech, the characteristic red color. The dark, almost black grain would be added with a brush. Such graining was frequently further embellished by the addition of fine black or white lines either running around the edge of the piece of furniture or along the center of its narrower parts, in imitation of ivory or ebony stringing, thereby adding crispness to the finish.

Picture frames – as long as their profile is simple with a surface uninterrupted by complicated moldings – make an ideal base for this kind of naive finish. Trays, boxes, and small pieces of furniture can be similarly treated.

TOOLS AND EQUIPMENT

Priming coat
White acrylic primer diluted with water to the consistency of light cream

Base coat
Brick-red vinyl silk latex

Glaze coat
Acrylic scumble tinted with black and burnt umber and diluted with water to the consistency of light cream

Antique finish
Satin finish acrylic varnish

Acrylic medium tinted with a little burnt umber

1½in/40mm brush
Fine sandpaper
1½in/40mm glider
Lint-free cloth

Level of skill required
Intermediate
Recommended on Furniture, picture frames, woodwork

ROSEWOOD GRAINING

a

Priming the surface
Using a 1½in/40mm brush, paint the picture frame with two to three coats of acrylic primer. Wait for each coat to dry, then sand with fine sandpaper to achieve a smooth and even surface.

Base coat
With the same brush, paint the picture frame with the base coat to a solid finish and let it dry completely.

Glaze coat
Using a 1½in/40mm glider, brush on the glaze coat along one side of the frame. Apply the glaze with a slightly tremulous motion of the hand to give the impression of the grain of the wood (**a**). Use a piece of lint-free cloth to wipe away any glaze that has been brushed over the miter (**b**).

Repeat for the other sides. The curve or sweep of the grain should vary from one side to the next. Be sure, before starting the fourth side, that the first is completely dry to avoid picking up paint from it.

c

b

Antique finish
For an antique effect, paint the frame with a coat of satin finish acrylic varnish. Follow with a glaze coat of tinted acrylic medium applied fairly unevenly. Finish with another coat of satin finish acrylic varnish (**c**).

Tortoiseshelling

Real tortoiseshell, when used as a veneer on small boxes and picture frames, is always backed, usually with paper. The backing is sometimes brightly colored and shows through the translucency of the shell, producing an exotic effect. Fake tortoiseshelling may be worked with different colored base coats to achieve similar effects. This example uses a straw-colored base for a natural tortoiseshell look. A particularly rich and effective alternative is to work the tortoiseshelling rather more densely over a rich vermilion base.

TOOLS AND EQUIPMENT

Priming coat
White acrylic primer diluted with water to the consistency of light cream

Base coat
White acrylic primer tinted with a little yellow ocher

Glaze coat
Yellow ocher gouache diluted with flat beer to a watery consistency

Tortoiseshell color
Burnt umber gouache diluted with flat beer to the consistency of light cream

Finish coats
White shellac
Acrylic varnish

1½in/40mm brush
Fine sandpaper
1½in/40mm glider
No.10 artists' brush
Lint-free cloth
Dusting brush or badger softener

Level of skill required Intermediate
Recommended on Small wooden objects such as boxes and picture frames

Priming

Using a 1½in/40mm brush, paint the picture frame with two to three coats of acrylic primer. Between coats, sand with fine sandpaper when dry to achieve a smooth and even surface.

Base coat

Apply the base coat with the same brush to a smooth finish.

Creating the tortoiseshell pattern

Using a 1½in/40mm glider, brush the glaze coat onto one section at a time (**a**). Immediately, while the glaze coat remains wet, use a No. 10 artists' brush to paint on the tortoiseshell color as shown, dabbing the color into the wet glaze coat (**b**).

a

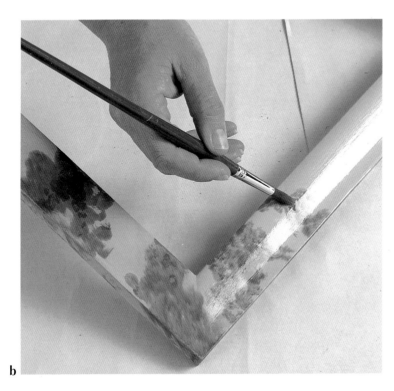

b

c

Softening the pattern

While the tortoiseshell color is still wet, soften its edges slightly into the glaze using a dry dusting brush or badger softener (**c**).
Apply some more of the tortoiseshell color to darken a few areas and soften their edges as before.

Protecting the surface

Apply two finish coats of white shellac followed by a coat of acrylic varnish if required.

Black and gold marbling

Much admired for its austerity, black and gold marbling was widely used in the nineteenth century on table tops and mantelpieces. The decorative effect was also applied to plinths for statues and to baseboards, where a solid black might be too heavy.

Here, the technique is used on the mat of a suitable and sympathetic print. It is important to choose heavy board, which will not warp as the paint dries. You can either buy a ready-colored black mat or paint a pale one black. A ready-colored board will still need to be sealed with acrylic medium before you apply further coats of paint.

TOOLS AND EQUIPMENT

Base coat
Black artists'
acrylic paint

Wash coat
Black and white
artists' acrylic paints,
mixed with at least
three times their
volume of acrylic
medium, and diluted
to a watery
consistency

First vein color
White artists' acrylic
paint mixed with a little
black and equal
quantities of acrylic
medium and water to
a watery consistency

Second vein color
Yellow ocher and white
artists' acrylic paints
mixed with twice their
volume of acrylic
medium and diluted to
a watery consistency

Final coat
Acrylic medium or varnish

1in/25mm brush
1½in/40mm glider
Palette, old plate, or jar lid
Fine, fine-to-medium, and medium lining brushes

Level of skill required Intermediate
Recommended on Small flat surfaces

Base coat
Using the 1in/25mm brush, paint the picture mat to a solid color with the base coat. The result should be smooth, so two thinned coats are better than one thicker coat. Let it dry completely.

Applying the wash coat
Use a 1½in/40mm glider to apply the first wash coat in two or three diagonal bands (**a**). Imagine the picture mat as a continuous piece of marble with a central hole, and keep the diagonal lines flowing from one side of the mount to the other.

Painting the veins
Mix a small quantity of the first vein color on a palette, old plate, or jar lid. With a medium lining brush filled with this color, lightly brush diagonal strokes across the picture mat, rolling the brush across the surface in places. Occasionally apply extra pressure to the brush to widen some of the veins to mimic real marble. Use a fine lining brush and the same color to add three or four more distinct veins (**b**).

a

b

Second vein color
Using a fine-to-medium lining brush, wash a very thin coat of the second, yellowish vein color over some, but not all, of the white veins (**c**).

Finishing
Finish with a coat of acrylic medium or varnish to give an even surface.

c

Pale marbling

Acrylic paint can be thinned to give a translucent glaze, making it particularly suitable for reproducing the translucent look of real marble. This sort of marbling using acrylic paint is very useful for painting small areas, such as fireplaces or furniture. It could also be used in preference to distemper for marbling in rooms where condensation might be a problem, such as kitchens and bathrooms.

In this example, two main colors are applied over the white base coat, but further layers could be added for extra depth. You could also change the color by washing a colored glaze over the finished marbling. In the marbling shown on pp128-9, acrylic glaze tinted with yellow ocher and burnt sienna, diluted with two-thirds water, has been washed over this gray and white marbling. Two glazes of different colors could, of course, be applied over a monochrome background to produce a more elaborate effect. If you adopt this technique to imitate colored marble, do not forget to remove some areas of the glaze as it dries to expose the paler marbling beneath, and to apply a second wash to give some areas of veining a richer color.

TOOLS AND EQUIPMENT

Base coat
White acrylic primer

First color
White acrylic primer tinted with raw umber and black, then mixed with an equal quantity of acrylic medium

Glaze coat
White acrylic primer and an equal quantity of acrylic medium

First vein color
First color plus a little more white acrylic primer

Second vein color
White artists' acrylic paint

Large decorators' brush
1½in/40mm brush
Flat-topped No.12 artists' brush
Lint-free cloth

Level of skill required
Advanced
Recommended on
Smooth wall surfaces, woodwork

a

Base coat
Using the large decorators' brush, paint the base coat to a solid finish and let it dry.

Applying the first color
Dip the 1½in/40mm brush in a little paint and apply it to the wall, then dip the brush in water and dilute the paint directly on the wall with a dabbing motion, brushing in all directions. The effect should be uneven patches of paint of different thicknesses (**a**). As the paint dries very quickly, work on only a small area at a time. Let it dry completely.

Applying the glaze coat
Paint the glaze coat using the 1½in/40mm brush, with a free and sweeping crisscross motion (**b**). Dilute the glaze coat with water as work proceeds. The glaze coat should produce a cloudy effect over the first color.

b

c

Painting the veins
With a flat-topped No.12 artists' brush, paint veins in the marble with the first vein color. Apply the paint in diagonal streaks with a slightly tremulous motion of the hand (**c**). Alter the pressure on the brush occasionally to produce variations in thickness.
Go over some of the veins several times to strengthen parts of the veining.

Painting the second vein color
Using the second vein color on the same brush, add some more veins. Roll the brush as it is drawn through the work to produce some thicker patches of veining, creating an irregular effect.

TOOLS AND EQUIPMENT

Base coat
White acrylic primer diluted with water to the consistency of light cream

Glaze coat
Acrylic medium tinted with yellow and yellow ocher and a little red and blue, then diluted with water to the consistency of thin milk

First paint color
Black artists' acrylic paint

Second paint color
Red and blue artists' acrylic paints diluted with water and acrylic medium in roughly equal proportions to a watery consistency

Shading color
First paint color diluted with water and acrylic medium in roughly equal proportions to a watery consistency

Top coat
Gloss acrylic varnish

Soft ½in/12mm or 1in/25mm brush
Fine pencil
Paper
Carbon paper
Ruler or straightedge
Fine lining brush
Medium artists' brush

Level of skill required Advanced
Recommended on Boxes, trays, small tables

Freestyle decoration

Eighteenth-century tea caddies provided the inspiration for the decoration on this box, which was carried out using acrylic paints and glazes. Always consider the suitability of the design to the shape of the object you are decorating. The central motif on this box lid was created to complement its octagonal shape, but a star shape might be a better choice for a square object, while a diamond could suit a rectangle. This simple form of freestyle decoration would also look good applied to a tray or small table.

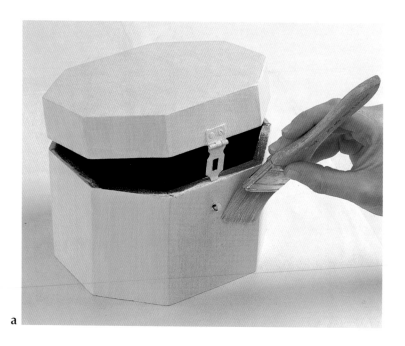

a

Painting the base colors
Use a soft ½in/12mm or 1in/25mm brush to paint the box to a solid color with three to four coats of white acrylic primer. Let each coat dry thoroughly before applying the next. Because the yellow glaze coats that follow are translucent, the primer should be applied carefully to create a very smooth and solid finish.

When the white primer is dry, use the same brush to apply four coats of the glaze (**a**). Because water-based paints dry so quickly, it is possible to build up an interesting translucent finish, with the white base coat still visible, without having to allow too much drying time between each coat. When applying subsequent layers of glaze, always brush in the same direction.

Planning the design

Plan the design for the box lid and draw it on paper to fit the box exactly. Plan a second design as a border to run around the top and bottom of the box and draw this to the required size on a piece of paper. The border design is continuous and does not need to be worked out separately for each face of the box.

Marking the design on the lid

Place the lid design on top of a piece of carbon paper on the box lid and, with a fine pencil, press lightly through the carbon paper, marking only the points where the curved lines of the design cross the straight axes (**b**). Mark these points as lightly as possible to avoid leaving heavy, paint-repelling carbon marks on the lid.

Drawing the lid design

Use the same fine pencil to join the points with freestyle curves (**c**). With the pencil and a ruler, join the points marking the straight axes.

b

d

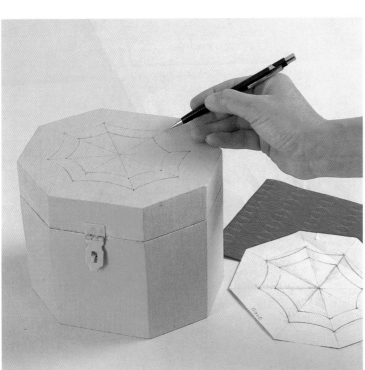

c

Marking the border design position

Hold the border design against the edge of the box and lightly mark in pencil the positions of each of the lines of the design at intervals around the box (**d**). Join the dots with a pencil, running the hand with the pencil along the edge of the box to maintain a constant distance from the edge. The center line marks the mid-line of the leafy band.

Painting the border design

With a fine lining brush and a ruler or straightedge to steady the hand, paint the straight lines of the border design around the edges of the box (**e**). For the thicker lines, apply more pressure to the brush.

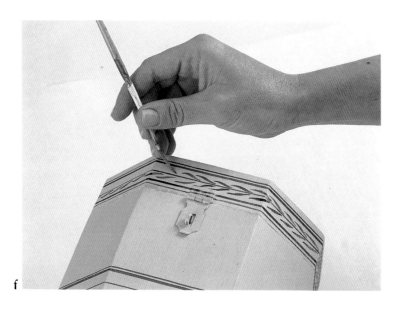

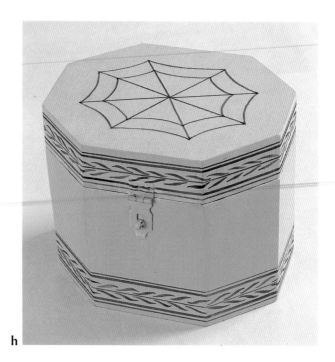

Painting the leaves

Use the fine lining brush to paint the leaves on each side of the line marking the center of the leafy band (**f**). Achieve a regular rhythm by painting the leaves on one side of the line at a time.

Start the base of each leaf with the point of the brush, then apply more pressure around the curve of the leaf, gradually reducing pressure to bring the brush to a point again at the tip of the leaf.

Painting the lid design

Using the fine lining brush and a straightedge or ruler, paint in the straight axes with the first paint color. Next, use the same brush and color to paint in the curved lines (**g** and **h**). Rest the free hand against the edge of the box and use it to support the hand holding the brush.

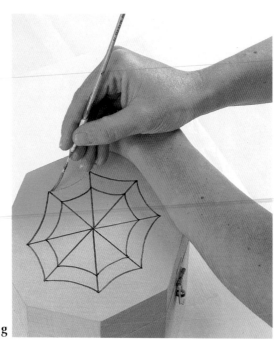

Shading the lid design

Use a medium artists' brush to paint the plum-colored band on top of the box with the second paint color. With a medium artists' brush and the shading glaze, paint bands of shading along one side of the straight axes on the top of the box. Apply a first narrow band of thin black shading glaze, then thin this glaze with more water, and apply a second, wider and paler band of shadow alongside and over the first (**i**).

Finishing

Add a final coat of gloss acrylic varnish to protect the painted pattern and give a glossy sheen to the box (**j**).

SUPPLIERS

Traditional and modern water-based products are available from many different sources. Many products are available in any paint shop but the list given here should help locate some of the less easily found items. The publishers would welcome suggestions for inclusion in this list and apologize in advance for any omissions.

USA AND CANADA

American Formulating and
Manufacturing (AFM)
350 West Ash Street
Suite 700
San Diego
CA 92101
Tel. 800 239 0321/619 239 0321

Supplier of paints formulated without toxic chemicals

Allsafe
5364 Pan American NE
Albuquerque
NM 87109
Tel. 505 881 2103

Supplier of paints formulated without toxic chemicals

Auro/Teekah Inc
5015 Yonge Street
North York
Ontario
Canada M2N 5PI
Tel. 416 229 4199

Distributor of Auro natural paints, including casein paints, latex paints, colorwash concentrates for application over latex paints, exterior masonry paints, shellacs, artists' and children's pure plant watercolors, color concentrates for tinting white latex, and chalk paint (an improved form of whitewash)

Best Paint Co
PO Box 3922
Seattle
WA 98124
Tel. 206 783 9938

Supplier of paints formulated without toxic chemicals

Binney & Smith Inc
1100 Church Lane
PO Box 431
Easton
PA 18044
Tel. 610 253 6271

Manufacturer of Liquitex Fine Art Products, including acrylic artists' colors in tubes or jars, acrylic medium and varnishes

Biofa, Bau Inc
PO Box 190
Alton
NH 03809
Tel. 603 226 3868

Manufacturer of natural paints and varnishes

General Finishes
PO Box 51567
New Berlin
WI 53151
Tel. 414 786 6050

Supplier of environmentally friendly, water-based staining systems, country colors, and clear finishes

Carver Tripp
Parks Corporation
One West Street
Fall River
MA 02720
Tel. 1 800 225 8543

Supplier of paints formulated without toxic chemicals

Eco-Design Company
1365 Rufina Circle
Santa Fe
NM 87501
Tel. 505 438 3448

Supplier of natural paints

Eco House (1988) Inc
Livos Plant Chemistry Canada
PO Box 220, Stn A Fredericton
New Brunswick
Canada E3B 4YN
Tel. 506 366 3529

Supplier of paints formulated without toxic chemicals

SUPPLIERS

Ecology Box
425 East Washington
Ann Arbor
MI 48101
Tel. 313 662 9131

Supplier of natural paints

Enviresource Inc
110 Madison Avenue North
Bainbridge Island
WA 98110
Tel. 206 842 9785

*Supplier of paints formulated without
toxic chemicals*

Frazee Paint and Wallcoverings
6625 Miramar Road
San Diego
CA 92121
Tel. 619 276 9500

*Supplier of paints formulated without
toxic chemicals*

Gryphin Co Inc
PO Box 5910
Philadelphia
PA 19137
Tel. 215 426 5976

*Manufacturer of the Heritage Village
Colors range of milk paint*

Mile High Crown Inc
DBA Crown Corporation NA
1801 Wynkop Street
Suite 235
Denver
CO 80202
Tel. 303 292 1313

*Manufacturer of vinyl matt and silk
latex*

The Old-Fashioned Milk Paint
Company Inc
PO Box 222
436 Main Street
Groton
MA 01450
Tel. 508 448 6336

*Manufacturer of genuine milk paint in
powder form*

Paint Magic
2426 Fillmore Street
San Francisco
CA 94115
Tel. 415 292 7780

*Manufacturer and supplier of Jocasta
Innes's Colorwash, Woodwash, Stencil
Paint, Historic Colors, Liming Paste
and Crackleglaze, as well as stencils,
rubber stamps, brushes and sponges*

Polyvine Limited
PO Box 538
Glastonbury
CT 06033
Tel. 203 633 0326

*Manufacturer and supplier of specialist
brushes, natural sponges, graining
combs, size, colorizers, acrylic scumble,
lacquer, crackle glaze and varnish*

Republic Paints
1128 North Highland Avenue
Hollywood
CA 90038
Tel. 213 957 3060

Supplier of latex

Shaker Shops West
PO Box 487
Inverness
CA 94937
Tel. 415 669 7256

Supplier of milk paint

Sinan Co
PO Box 857
Davis
CA 95617
Tel. 916 753 3104

Distributor of Auro natural paints

The Stulb Company
PO Box 597
Allentown
PA 18105
Tel. 1 800 221 8444

*Manufacturer of the Williamsburg
Buttermilk Paint Colors range*

W.M. Zinsser & Co Inc
173 Belmont Drive
Somerset
NJ 08875
Tel. 602 460 5343

*Manufacturer of shellac, shellac base,
and other decorating specialities*

Winsor and Newton Inc
11 Constitution Avenue
PO Box 1396
Piscataway
NJ 08855
Tel. 908 562 0770

*Manufacturer of size, powder pigments,
poster colors, artists' acrylic colors,
acrylic medium and varnish, designers'
gouache colors, and artists' brushes*

UNITED KINGDOM

Acrylon Environmental Ltd
PO Box 684
Amersham
Buckinghamshire HP6 6DX
Tel. 1494 726890

Supplier and manufacturer of water-borne coatings for rusty metal, clean metal, galvanized steel, fiberglass, masonry, and wood

J.W. Bollom
PO Box 78
Croydon Road
Beckenham
Kent BR3 4BL
Tel. 181 6582299

Supplier and manufacturer of latex, vinyl sheen latex, Bromel vinyl latex (a trade range available as vinyl matt or vinyl silk), the Hydrocote range (a range of water-based wood-finishing products including a lacquer, a sealer, a primer and a finish coat, and woodstainers), Bromel Aquastone Masonry Paint (an acrylic-based exterior masonry paint), acrylic scumbles, glazes, medium, and varnishes

Craig & Rose plc
172 Leith Walk
Edinburgh EH6 5EB
Tel. 1322 222481

Manufacturer and supplier of acrylic scumbles, varnishes, medium, and glazes

Cy-Près
14 Bells Close
Brigstock
Kettering
Northamptonshire NN14 3JG
Tel. 1536 373431

Manufacturer and supplier of limewash and soft distemper

The English Stamp Company
Sunnydown
North Matravers
Dorset BH19 3JP
Tel. 1929 439117
Manufacturer and supplier of rubber stamps

Farrow & Ball Ltd
33 Uddens Trading Estate
Wimborne
Dorset BH21 7NL
Tel. 1202 876141

Manufacturer and supplier of limewash, soft distemper, oil-bound distemper, latex , and water stainers; manufacturer of the National Trust paint range

Fired Earth plc
Twyford Mill
Oxford Road
Adderbury
Oxfordshire OX17 3HP
Tel. 1295 812088

Manufacturer and supplier of distemper and latex

Grand Illusions
2-4 Crown Road
St Margarets
Twickenham
Middlesex TW1 3EE
Tel. 181 744 1046

Manufacturer and supplier of an acrylic-based water-soluble paint suitable for wood or walls that emulates traditional milk paint

Hall, Whorrell & Moon
12 Latham Street
Brigstock
Kettering
Northamptonshire NN14 3HD
Tel. 1536 373001

Manufacturer and supplier of limewash, soft distemper, oil-bound distemper, and shellac

ICI Paints
Wexham Road
Slough
Berkshire SL2 5DS
Tel. 1753 550000

Manufacturer of a range of Dulux vinyl matt and vinyl silk latex paints, Weathershield Smooth and Textured Masonry Paint, Weathershield Aquatech Woodstain, Quick-Drying Floor Paint, Quick-Drying Acrylic Metal Primer, Quick-Drying Gloss, and Quick-Drying Eggshell

Liberon
Mountfield Industrial Estate
New Romney
Kent TN28 8XU
Tel. 1797 367555

Manufacturer and supplier of the acrylic-based products Palette Wood Dye, Wood Decor Varnish and Exterior Woodwork Finish, also shellac and artists' brushes

Macpherson Paints Ltd
PO Box 60
Abingdon
Oxfordshire OX14 4UQ
Tel. 1235 862226

Manufacturer of vinyl matt and vinyl silk latex , acrylic basecoat, gloss and eggshell paints, Aquaflek, Aquatone and Aquaroll water-borne multicolor paint finishes

Nutshell Natural Paints
Newtake
Staverton
Devon TQ9 6PE
Tel. 1803 762329

Manufacturer and supplier of milk paint, and earth and mineral pigments

Papers and Paints
4 Park Walk
London SW10 OAD
Tel 171 352 8626

Supplier of limewash, distemper, milk and latex paints, quick-drying gloss, eggshell and masonry paints, decorators' and artists' brushes, graining combs and stipplers, artists' acrylic paints, acrylic varnishes, scumbles and medium, dry pigments and stainers, shellac, glue size, whiting, and stencilling materials

Potmolen Paint
27 Woodcock Industrial Estate
Warminster
Wiltshire BA12 9DX
Tel. 1985 213960

Manufacturer and supplier of casein paints, glue size, whiting, limewashes, soft distemper, oil-bound distemper, pigment wash (to wash over distemper and some synthetic water-based paints), Linstain wood stains, decorators' and artists' brushes, gold leaf, shellac, and pigments

Relics
35 Bridge Street
Witney
Oxfordshire OX8 6DA
Tel. 1993 704611

UK main distributor for Annie Sloan's Traditional Paints, a range of water-based paints that mimic the appearance of distemper, limewash, and milk paint

Rose of Jericho
Westhill Barn
Evershot
Dorchester
Dorset DT2 0LD
Tel. 1935 83676/83662

Manufacturer and supplier of milk paint, limewashes, soft distemper, oil-bound distemper, and claircolle, a traditional primer/undercoat for soft distemper

Spectrum
259 Queens Road
Wimbledon
London SW19 8NY
Tel. 181 542 4729

Manufacturer of artists' acrylic colors

The Stencil Library
Stocksfield Hall
Stocksfield
Northumberland NE43 7TN
Tel. 1661 844844

Stencil designs and stencilling equipment by mail order

SUPPLIERS' CREDITS

The publishers would like to thank the following companies who donated paints and other materials, or lent items for special photography.

MATERIALS

Acrylon Environmental Ltd, PO Box 684, Amersham, Buckinghamshire HP6 6DX, England. Tel. 1494 726890

Cornelissen & Son Ltd, 105 Great Russell Street, London WC1B 3RY, England. Tel. 171 6361045

The English Stamp Company, Sunnydown, Worth Matravers, Dorset BH19 3JP, England. Tel. 1929 439117

Farrow & Ball Ltd (manufacturer of the National Trust paint range), 33 Uddens Trading Estate, Wimborne, Dorset BH21 7NL, England. Tel. 1202 876141

Grand Illusions, 2-4 Crown Road, St Margarets, Middlesex TW1 3EE, England. Tel. 181 7441046

Papers and Paints, 4 Park Walk, London SW10 0AD, England. Tel. 171 352 8626

ACCESSORIES

Page 77 Pomegranate wreath, nutmeg wreath and gingerbread girl from Appalachia, 14a George Street, St Albans, Herts AL3 4ER, England. Tel. 1727 836796

Page 78 Shelves, mirror, starfish and wooden boat from Pretty Arty, 20 Lower King's Road, Berkhamsted, Herts HP4 2AB, England. Tel. 1442 878939

Page 81 Picture and cream throw from Appalachia (see above). Patterned throw from Pretty Arty (see above).

Page 87 Teddy bear from Appalachia (see above).

Pages 136 and 138 Candlesticks from Scumble Goosie, 1 Cotswold Place, Chalford Hill, Stroud, Gloucestershire GL6 8EJ, England. Tel. 1453 886414

BIBLIOGRAPHY

J. Ayres *The Artist's Craft* Phaidon, London, 1985

R.D. Harley *Artists' Pigments c.1600-1835* Butterworth Scientific, London, 2nd ed., 1982

Home Mechanic Series: Painting and Decorating Pearson, London, 1947

Jocasta Innes *The New Paint Magic* Frances Lincoln, London/ Pantheon, New York, 1992

J. Lawrence *Painting from A to Z* Sutherland, Manchester, 2nd ed. 1938

Ralph Mayer *The Artist's Handbook of Materials and Techniques* Faber & Faber, London/Viking, New York, 3rd ed. 1973

Judith and Martin Miller *Period Finishes and Effects* Mitchell Beazley, London/Rizzoli, New York, 1992

Isabel O'Neil *The Art of the Painted Finish for Furniture and Decoration* William, Morrow & Co., New York, 1971

John P. Parry *Modern Techniques in Painting and Decorating* Longman, London, 1950

W.L. Savage *Practical House Decoration* Austin Rogers & Co., London, 1927

John Sutcliffe *Decorating Magic* Frances Lincoln, London/ Pantheon, New York, 1994

Nathaniel Whittock *The Decorative Painters' and Glaziers' Guide* Isaac Taylor Hinton, London, 1827

Michael Wilcox *The Wilcox Guide to the Finest Watercolour Paints* Artways, Perth, 1991

Michael Wilcox *Blue and Yellow Don't Make Green* Collins, London/North Light, Cincinatti, 1989

ARTICLES AND FACTSHEETS

Robert Butcher *A Case for Traditional and Natural Paints and Coatings* Society for the Protection of Ancient Buildings News, Vol. 14, No. 2, 1993

Dulux Factsheet No.1 *Dulux Decorative Environmental Policy*

Dulux Factsheet No.2 *Why Use Water-based Paints?*

Dulux Factsheet No.3 *Paint and the Environment*

Dulux Factsheet No.4 *Handy Tips When Painting With Dulux*

Dulux Factsheet No.5 *How to Remove Old Paint Containing Lead Safely*

How Green is my Front Door? B & Q's Second Environmental Review, 1995

Roy Miller *Safer Paint* Architects' Journal, July 1992

INDEX

Page numbers in *italic* refer to illustrations

acrylic gold size 138, *139*
acrylic medium 15, 130
  added to distemper 43
acrylic paints 128-59
  antiquing 140-1, *140-1*
  binders 14
  black and gold marbling 152-3, *152-3*
  bronzed finish 138-9, *138-9*
  colorwashing 140-1, *140-1*
  combing 142-3, *142-3*
  freestyle decoration 156-9, *156-9*
  marbling 58
  on ferrous metals 134-5, *134-5*
  pale marbling 154-5, *154-5*
  pigments 14, 15
  rosewood graining 148-9, *148-9*
  stippling 142-3, *142-3*
  tortoiseshelling 150-1, *150-1*
  verdigris effect 136-7, *136-7*
acrylic polymers 96, 130
acrylic primer 33, 36, 96
acrylic scumble 130-3
air pollution 7
alizarin crimson *17*
aniline black 26
antiquing 140-1, *140-1*
artists' paints 128-59
  mahogany graining 144-7, *146-7*
  oak graining 144-5, *144-5*
azurite 21

badger softener 39, *39*
bamboo 36
bathrooms *32, 131*
binders 7, 14, 15
black chalk 26
black pigments 26

blue pigments 20-1
blue verditer 21
body color 133
bone black 26
bronzed finish 138-9, *138-9*
brown ocher 24
brown pigments 24-5
brushes 38
burnt sienna 25, *25*
burnt umber *24, 25*

cadmium red 17
cadmium yellow 19, *19*
cane furniture 36
caraway oil, milk paints 72
carbon black 26
carmine 17
carpenter's level 39, *39*
casein 14, 15
  milk paints 72
ceiling molding, removing paint 30
ceilings
  order of painting 34
  stripping 33
cerulean blue *21*
ceruse 27
chairs *132*
  freestyle detail 90-3, *90-3*
chalk 27, *27*
chalk line 39, *39*
checks, freestyle 112-13, *112-13*
Chinese ink 26
Chinese white 27
Chinese yellow 19
chrome yellow 19
cleaning surfaces 30
clearing the room 30
cobalt *20, 21*
colors
  color wheel 12
  complementary 12
  contrasting 12, 13
  cool 12

darkening 13
lightening 13
mixing 12-13
testing 15
theory of 12-13
tints 13
tones 13
warm 12
colorwashing
  acrylic 140-1, *140-1*
  distemper 43-46, *46-9*
  latex 97, 100, *100-3*
  over sponging 104-5, *104-7*
combing, acrylics 142-3, *142-3*
complementary colors 12
contract latex 96
contrasting colors 13, *13*
cool colors 12
cornices
  order of painting 34
  removing old paint 30
covering power 15
cutting stencils 83, 86, 118
cutting in 34

dado 34, 66, 118
damask effects 120, *121*
damp surfaces 43, 96
Danish oil 77
darkening colors 13
decoration
  freestyle detail 90-3, *90-3*, 156-9, *156-9*
  freestyle painted garland 66-9, *66-9*
  freestyle stripes and checks 112-13, *112-13*
  gilding 138, *139*
  painted stenciling 118-19, *118-19*
  rubber stamping 78-9, *78-9*
  sponge stamping 62-5, *62-5*
  sponged stripes 110-11, *110-11*
  stenciling on wood 86-9, *86-9*

trompe l'oeil tiles 124-7, *125-7*
  wall stenciling 80-5, *80-5*, 120-21, *120-21*
Delft tile effect 125
dilution, translucency and 15
distemper 7, 30, 33, 40-69
  binders 14
  coloring 14, 43
  colorwashing 46-9, *46-9*
  freestyle painted garland 66-9, *66-9*
  limewash 44, 72
  mixing 43
  oil-bound 33, 44, 46, 54, 58, 62, 66
  over latex 46
  painting over 30
  priming 33
  removing 30
  soft 43, 46, 50, 52
  spattering 52-3, *52-3*
  sponge stamping 62-5, *62-5*
  sponging 50-1, *50-1*
  trompe l'oeil stone blocks 54-7, *54-7*
distressed effect, on wood 114, *114-15*
doors, paneled 36
drying time, stainers 14

Egyptian brown 25
emerald green 22
equipment 38-9

ferrous metals
  acrylic paints on 134-5, *134-5*
  latex on 96
filling holes 33
finishes
  antiquing 140-1, *140-1*
  black and gold marbling 152-3, *152-3*
  bronze effect 138-9, *138-9*

colorwashes over sponging 104-5, *104-7*
combing 142-3, *142-3*
distemper colorwashes 46, *46-9*
distressed wood 114, *114-15*
flat painting 76-7, *76-7*
simple and layered sponging 108, *108-9*
latex colorwashes 100, *100-3*
mahogany graining 146-7, *146-7*
oak graining 144-5, *144-5*
pale marbling 154-5, *154-5*
pickled wood *116-17*, 117
rosewood graining 148-9, *148-9*
spattering 52-3, *52-3*
sponged stripes 110-11, *110-11*
sponging 50-1, *50-1*
stenciling 80-9, 118-23
stippling 142-3, *142-3*
tortoiseshelling 150-1, *150-1*
trompe l'oeil stone blocks 54-7, *54-7*
verdigris 136-7, *136-7*
fitch 39, *39*
flat painting 76-7, *76-7*
foam roller 39, *39*
freestyle painting
acrylics 156-9, *156-9*
latex 112-13, *112-13*
milk paint 90-3, *90-3*
frit 20
furniture 36
antiquing 140-1, *140-1*
combing 142-3, *142-3*
distressed effect 114, *114-15*
freestyle detail 90-3, *90-3*
graining 143
mahogany graining 144-7, *146-7*

oak graining 144-5, *144-5*
outdoor *132*
primed 37
rosewood graining 148-9, *148-9*
stippling 142-3, *142-3*
tortoiseshelling 150-1, *150-1*

gamboge 18, *18*
garland, freestyle painted 66-9, *66-9*
gilding 138, *139*
glazes
coloring 15
milk paints 72
verdigris effect 136-7, *136-7*
glider 39, *39*
gloss paint, painting over 33
gold leaf and size 138, *139*
gouache 15, 133, 144, 146, 150
graining 143
mahogany 146-7, *146-7*
oak 144-5, *144-5*
rosewood 148-9, *149-9*
granite effect, sponging 50-1, *50-1*
green earth 22, *22*
green pigments 22-3
green verditer 22
grids, stenciling 83

India ink 26
Indian lake 17
Indian red 16, *16*, 17
Indian yellow 18
indigo 20, *21*
iron
acrylic paints on 130
latex paint on 96, *134-5*
ivory black 26

knotting 33

lamp black 26
adding to paint 14

lapis lazuli 20-1, *20*
latex 94-127
binders 14, 96
colorwashing over sponging 104-5, *104-7*
contract 96
distemper painted over 46
distressing wood 114, *114-15*
freestyle stripes and checks 112-13, *112-13*
layered sponging 108, *108-9*
overpainting 46, 96
painted stenciling 118-19, *118-19*
pickled wood *116-17*, 117
removing 30
simple color washing 100, *100-3*
sponge stenciling 120-3, *120-3*
sponging stripes 110-11, *110-11*
trompe l'oeil tiles 124-7, *125-7*
layered sponging 108, *108-9*
lead antimolliate 19
lead paints 7, 14
lemon yellow 18, 19
lightening colors 13
limewash 27, 72
using 44, *116-17*, 117
lining fitch 39, *39*
linseed oil
binders 14
distemper 44
milk paints 72
lithopone 27

madder 17
mahogany graining 146-7, *146-7*
malachite 22, *22*
marble effects
black and gold 152-3, *152-3*
marbling 58-9, *58-61*
pale 154-5, *154-5*

Mars black 26
Mars brown 25
Mars yellow 18
masking tape, sponged stripes 110, 111
matte latex 96
measuring stencils 86
metal, acrylic paints 130, 134-5, *134-5*
milk paints 70-93
binders 14
flat painting 76-7, *76-7*
freestyle details 90-3, *90-3*
mildew 72
painting over 72
primers 33
rubber stamping 78-9, *78-9*
stenciling 72, *73*
stenciling on walls 80-5, *80-5*
stenciling on wood 86-9, *86-9*
mildew, milk paints 72
mixing paint, adding color 14-15

Naples yellow 19
nut oil, milk paints 72

oak graining 144-5, *144-5*
ochers 24
oil-based paints 8
oil-bound distemper 33, 44, 46, 54, 58, 62, 66
opacity 15
order of painting 34-6, *35*
orpiment 19
ozone layer 7

paint stripping
ceiling molding 30
ceilings 33
cornices 30
furniture 36
walls 33
paints
acrylic 128-59

INDEX

artists' paints 128-59
binders 7, 14, 15
contract latex 96
distemper 7, 40-69
gouache 15, 133, 144, 146, 150
latex 94-127
milk paints 70-93
oil-based 8
pigments 14, 15, 16-27
poster paint 14, 15, 133
primers 33
waste paint 7
water-based paints 7-8
paneled doors 36
paper, stripping 30-3
papier-mâché 36
Paris green 23
patent yellow 19
patina effect, verdigris 136-7
phthalocyanine blue 21, 21
phthalocyanine green 22, 23
pickled wood 116-17, 117
pigments 7, 8
acrylics 15
adding color to paint 14
black 26
blue 20-1
brown 24-5
covering power 15
gouache 15
green 22-3
poster paints 15
powder colors 15
pure 14
pure pigments 14
red 16-17
stainers 14
white 27
yellow 18-19
pollution 7
polymers see acrylic paints
porphyry, imitating 52
poster paint 14, 15, 133
powder color 14, 15
preparation 30-3
cleaning the surfaces 30

clearing the room 30
furniture 36
priming surfaces 33
removing paint and paper 30-3
smoothing the surface 33
primary colors 12
printer's black 26
Prussian blue 21, 21

raw sienna 25, 25
raw umber 24, 24
red lead 17
red pigments 16-17
rosewood graining 148-9, 148-9
rubber stamping, milk paints 78-9

saffron 18
sap green 23
sash windows 36
Scheele's green 23
Schweinfurt green 23
scumble, acrylic 130-3
secondary colors 12
sepia 25, 25
shellac 33
size, binders 14, 15
smell 7
soft distemper 43, 46, 50, 52
solvents, pollution 7-8
soot 26
Spanish white 27
spattering 52-3, 52-3
sponges
stamping 62-5, 62-5
stenciling 120-3, 120-3
sponging 44, 50-1, 50-1
colorwashes over 104-5, 104-7
layered 108, 108-9
stripes 110-11, 110-11
stainers 14
stamping
milk paints 78-9, 78-9
sponge 62-5, 62-5

steel
acrylic paints 130, 134-5, 134-5
latex paint on 96
stencil brush 39, 39
stenciling
cutting stencils 83, 86, 118
milk paints 72, 73
painted 118-19, 118-19
sponge 120-3, 120-3
walls 80-5, 80-5
on wood 86-9, 86-9
stippler 39, 39
stippling, acrylics 142-3, 142-3
stone blocks, fake 54-7, 54-7
stripes
freestyle 112-13, 112-13
sponging 110-11, 110-11
stripping
ceiling molding 30
ceilings 33
cornices 30
furniture 36
walls 33
surfaces, preparing 30-3

terre verte 22, 22
testing colors 15
tiles, trompe l'oeil 124-7, 125-7
tints 13
titanium white 27
tones 13
tortoiseshelling 150-1, 150-1
toxic pigments 14
translucency 15
trompe l'oeil
stone blocks 54-7, 54-7
tiles 124-7, 125-7
Turner's yellow 19
two-stage sponge stamping 62-5, 62-5

ultramarine 20-1, 20
umber 24
universal stainers 14

Vandyke brown 25
Venetian lake 17
Venetian red 16, 17
verdigris 22, 23, 136-7, 136-7
vermilion 17, 17
vine black 26
vinyl polymers 96
viridian 23
volatile organic compounds (VOCs) 7

walls
order of painting 34
stripping 33
warm colors 12
waste paint 7
water stainers 14
water-based paints, advantages of 7-8
white chalk 27, 27
white lead 27
white pigments 27
whiting 27, 43
wicker furniture 36
windows 36
wood and woodwork
antiquing 140-1, 140-1
distressed effect 114, 114-15
mahogany graining 144-7, 146-7
milk paints 74, 76
oak graining 114-15, 144-5
order of painting 34
outdoor furniture 132
preparing 33
rosewood graining 148-9, 148-9
stenciling on 86-9, 86-9
stripping 30
tortoiseshelling 150-1, 150-1

yellow ocher 18, 18
yellow pigments 18-19

zinc oxide 27

ACKNOWLEDGMENTS

AUTHOR'S ACKNOWLEDGMENTS

I should like to thank all the friends, clients and colleagues who have, over the years, encouraged me in the use of water-based paints. I should also like to thank Hilary Mandleberg and everyone who has helped with the production of this book, namely the staff at Frances Lincoln, especially James Bennett, Caroline Bugler, Anne Fraser and Anne Wilson, and the photographer Andrew Twort and his assistant Deborah Murray.

I would also like to thank: The American Museum in Britain, Claverton Manor, Bath; John Ashworth of ECOS paints; Stephen Barclay of Shaker Kitchens; Patrick Baty, for advice and help over the years and access to his B.A. dissertation for the University of East London 'The Methods and Materials of the House-Painter in England: An Analysis of House-Painting Literature, 1660-1850'; Derek C. Coe of Acrylon Environmental Ltd; David Crowther; The Department of Trade and Industry's Environmental Helpline; Friends of the Earth; Tom Helme and Martin Ephson of Farrow & Ball for their generosity; Mr Johnston, Levi Strauss (UK) Ltd; London Waste Regulation Authority; National Household Hazardous Waste Forum; Emma Pearce of Winsor & Newton; Hank Topper of the U.S. Environmental Protection Agency; Keith Warwick of Polyvine; John Wright, Dulux Technical Department, I.C.I. Paints. I am also indebted to Dr Ian Bristow for access to his thesis 'Interior House-painting from the Restoration to the Regency' and acknowledge the use I have made of this.

PUBLISHER'S ACKNOWLEDGMENTS

Frances Lincoln Publishers would like to thank Hilary Bird for supplying the index, and Barry Christian, Louise Cox, Fred Gill, Maggi McCormick and Eva Wolpert for their help with the book.

Editor Caroline Bugler
Assistant Editor James Bennett
Editorial Director Erica Hunningher
Art Director Caroline Hillier
Picture Researcher Sue Gladstone
Head of Pictures Anne Fraser
Production Jennifer Cohen

PHOTOGRAPHIC ACKNOWLEDGMENTS

All photographs by Andrew Twort © FLL except those listed below:

PAGE

2   Andreas von Einsiedel (designer Maurice Savinel)
4-5   Tim Ridley © FLL
6   Simon Upton/Elizabeth Whiting and Associates
8-9   Lena Koller/*Sköna Hem*/Camera Press
32   Nadia Mackenzie/*Country Homes & Interiors*/Robert Harding Syndication
34-35   Lena Koller/*Sköna Hem*/Camera Press
40-41   Tim Ridley © FLL
42   Jan Verlinde (designer Pieter Vandenhout)
44   *The World of Interiors*/René Stoeltie
45   Ianthe Ruthven (designer Rolf Blakstad)
47   Jan Verlinde (designer Pieter Vandenhout)
54   Andreas von Einsiedel (artist Michael Daly)
55   Andreas von Einsiedel (artist Michael Daly, designer Monika Apponyi)
58   Paul Ryan/International Interiors
60-61   Paul Ryan/International Interiors
73   Courtesy of the Shelburne Museum, Shelburne, Vermont/Ken Burris
74   Ianthe Ruthven
75   Bernard Touillon/*Côté Sud*/Elizabeth Whiting and Associates
80   Courtesy of The American Museum in Britain, Bath
97   Lena Koller/*Sköna Hem*/Camera Press
98   Paul Ryan/International Interiors (designer Jo Nahem)
99   Paul Ryan/International Interiors (designer Kathy Gallagher)
102-3   Peter Woloszynski/The Interior Archive Ltd
106   Roland Beaufre/Agence Top (architect Stuart Church)
115   Ulf Rennéus/*Sköna Hem*/IMS
116   Fritz von der Schulenburg/The Interior Archive Ltd (designer Mimmi O'Connell)
131   Andreas von Einsiedel (designer Frédéric Mechiche)
132   Jan Tham/*Sköna Hem*/Camera Press
133   Ianthe Ruthven (artists Matthew and Maro Spender)